# A Guide to Youth Ministry

Exploring the needs of your church

# A Guide to Youth Ministry

Exploring the needs of your church

**Katie McDaniel**

National Society/Church House Publishing

Church House

Great Smith Street

London SW1P 3NZ

ISBN 0 7151 4928 8

Published 1999 by the National Society (Church of England) for Promoting Religious Education and Church House Publishing

Cover design by Leigh Hurlock, Hurlock Design

Printed in England by The Cromwell Press Ltd, Trowbridge, Wiltshire

# Contents

# Acknowledgements

The author and publisher gratefully acknowledge permission to reproduce copyright material in this book. Every effort has been made to trace and contact copyright holders. If there are any inadvertent omissions we apologize to those concerned and will ensure that a suitable acknowledgement is made at the next reprint.

'Congregation questionnaire on youth work' (p. 11), 'Young people and the church' (p. 12), 'Treasured moments' (p. 65), 'Food' (p. 66), 'Affirmation' (p.67) and 'Light a candle' (p. 67) are taken from the *Youth A Part Resources Pack*, National Society/Church House Publishing, 1996. Copyright © 1996 The Archbishops' Council and used with permission.

'Three youth ministry models' (p. 19) and 'My evaluation of our church's youth ministry right now' (pp. 86–8) are reprinted by permission from Thom and Joani Schultz, *Kids Taking Charge: Youth-led Youth Ministry,* copyright © 1987, by Thom and Joani Schultz, published by Group Publishing, Inc., PO Box 481, Loveland, CO 80539.

'Guidelines for starting conversations' (p. 31) is reprinted by permission from Dr Barbara B. Varenhorst and Lee Sparks, *Training Teenagers for Peer Ministry*, copyright © 1988, by Dr Barbara B. Varenhorst and Lee Sparks, published by Group Publishing, Inc., PO Box 481, Loveland, CO 80539.

'Inappropriate relationships' (p. 32) is reprinted by permission from Dana A. Max, *Right Roles and Relationships in Youth Ministry*, unpublished manuscript, 1997 and is copyright © 1997 Dana A. Max.

'Just walk with me' (p. 41) and 'Where are we going' (p. 82, adapted) are taken from training materials provided by the Institute for Professional Youth Ministry.

Appendix 1, 'Safe from Harm: Summary of recommendations' (p. 100) is copyright © Crown. Crown copyright material is reproduced with the permission of the Controller of Her Majesty's Stationery Office.

The consent forms in Appendix 2, 'General Information and Consent', 'Activities and Day Visits', and 'Hazardous Activities' (pp. 100–102) are copyright © Trustees for Methodist Church Purposes and used by permission of Methodist Publishing House.

# Note on Photocopying

# Introduction

This book has a very simple purpose – to help any church develop a professional youth ministry that is totally realistic and appropriate for their circumstances. It is not a book of resources designed to embellish an existing youth group programme or a theoretical text on the nature of youth ministry. Rather it is a practical route through the questions and discussions that will take any church into a realistic, solidly founded, church-owned and supported response to young people.

In my work as Diocesan Youth Officer for the Church of England Diocese of Canterbury, I worked with many parishes wishing to respond to the needs of the young people with whom they were in contact, or whom they knew to be part of the parish, but who were totally unconnected with the church. It is my firm belief and experience that the skills, wisdom and knowledge to engage in successful youth ministry exist within every church. This book simply offers a way into using existing expertise in the most appropriate way for your church.

Whilst it is helpful to learn from what other churches have done (and there are several real examples of different churches' youth ministries throughout this book), the most successful youth ministry can only be what is wholly appropriate and realistically sustainable for your church. The message of this book is very simple: that it is better to do one thing well and build on it, than attempt an enormous programme without first laying solid foundations. I have seen many churches respond to the young people in their midst, or to the lack of them, in a hasty panic. This is commonly out of a realization that there is little or no provision for young people and a desire to do something rather than nothing. Unfortunately, poorly established youth ministry can do more harm than good, often resulting in isolation, burnout, ill feelings, bad practice and, at worst, a long-term reluctance to engage in any form of youth ministry again.

In this book you will find nine chapters on different aspects of youth ministry, each accompanied by an **action summary**, an **evaluation tool** and a **session outline** for use within the church. These session outlines can either be used independently to explore the particular chapter topic, say in a church council meeting, or as an eight-part course exploring youth ministry.

Prior to my full-time diocesan position, I worked as the part-time youth minister for a team ministry and trained through an internship at the Institute for Professional Youth Ministry, USA – a two-year in-service course for professional, paid youth ministers. My role in Canterbury Diocese was then to establish an equivalent training course: the Youth Ministry Training Programme, whose aim is to provide in-service training for those working in youth ministry, based on the belief that the professional standards required and the areas of skill and knowledge needed are the same whether people are working in a paid or voluntary capacity. The nine chapters in this book are drawn from the Institute for Professional Youth Ministry and the Youth Ministry Training Programme and offered in order that your church may develop a professional ministry with young people.

It is not intended that the book will provide you with a step-by-step recipe for a youth ministry programme, but rather that it will help you think in a logical and objective way about how your church can establish a youth ministry – a response to young people – that is totally appropriate, highly professional and wholly sustainable for you.

*Katie McDaniel*

# Distribution List

When you have finished reading this book,
please pass it on to the next person on the list below.
Thank you!

| Name | Address | Please tick when read |
|---|---|---|
| Vicar | | |
| Curate | | |
| Churchwarden | | |
| Churchwarden | | |
| Youth Group Leader | | |
| Youth Group Leader | | |
| Sunday School Leader | | |
| Sunday School Leader | | |
| Young People: | | |
| | | |
| | | |
| | | |
| | | |
| | | |
| Parents: | | |
| | | |
| | | |
| | | |
| | | |
| Church Council Members: | | |
| | | |
| | | |
| | | |
| | | |
| | | |
| | | |

# Setting Out

## About this book

You are probably reading this book because you have some young people in your church, or maybe you would like to encourage some to come along. Congratulations – you have taken the first step in engaging with young people! Recent statistics show that only one third of churches have any sort of involvement with young people. For some this may be through an organized youth group or activity; for others young people may be members of the congregation, in the choir or servers at the Eucharist. Yet for other churches young people are an age group they feel they can only dream of engaging with.

An active youth ministry *is* a realistic possibility for *any* church, provided that the church is prepared for it!

Youth ministry is fundamental to the ministry of any church, not simply as growth potential for the congregation but because young people are the here and now as well as the future. Young people constitute one third of the world's population. How many churches can honestly say that their ministry, their budgeting, their time, their people power invest one third of their energies into young people? Youth ministry presents a challenge to the Church because it calls for the Church to be inclusive of young people, to offer a special ministry to fulfil this inclusivity and yet not to be ageist in its approach or to compartmentalize young people.

This book will help your church to prepare realistically to meet this challenge by leading you through an exploration of what youth ministry could and should be for your particular church. In the following eight chapters we will ask some of the fundamental questions that will help you determine and shape your own youth ministry. You will find further points for consideration and, where appropriate, reports on the experiences of other churches.

At the end of each chapter you will also find a suggested **session outline**, which offers a format for initiating discussion within the church. You may find it useful to take these eight session outlines and use them as a dedicated eight-part training and development programme for your church, or you may wish to use them independently as the need arises.

Either way, this book is designed to help you:

- get to grips with what youth ministry can be;

- create a vision of youth ministry for your church;

- develop a youth ministry that is realistic, professional and sustainable;

- continue to monitor and evaluate your youth ministry.

This book offers you the questions that you will need to answer as a church. It will also offer you supportive information, ideas and real life examples. It will not offer you prescriptive answers or a specific formula but will enable your church to shape a ministry that is wholly appropriate and sustainable for you.

The book covers the following topics:

## Chapter 2    What is youth ministry?

This chapter will help you:

- come to an understanding of what youth ministry is;

- build a vision of a youth ministry that is relevant and appropriate for your church;

- prepare to take action.

## Chapter 3    The team approach

This chapter will help you:

- explore and become comfortable with the concept of a team approach;

- build and maintain a volunteer team;

- understand the implications of good practice and child protection for voluntary youth work.

## Chapter 4    Relational ministry

This chapter will help you:

- begin to explore the concept of relational ministry;

- build a strategic approach to developing relationships;

- revisit basic listening skills;

- consider how to develop appropriate, healthy relationships.

## Chapter 5    Using groups

This chapter will help you:

- identify some of the options;

- consider what would suit your church;

- prepare and plan for a youth-group meeting – setting goals, aims and objectives;

- think through resources available to you;

- evaluate your progress.

## Chapter 6    Responding to families

This chapter will help you:

- explore how a youth ministry can embrace a young person's family situation;

explore how to keep families informed, involved and supported.

## Chapter 7    Young people and worship

This chapter will ask you:

- What are our young people's needs from worship?

- How does that fit in with our existing worship?

- How can the two come together?

## Chapter 8    Peer ministry

This chapter will help you:

- explore the philosophy of youth ministry;

- consider when and why peer ministry can fail;

- begin to develop your own peer ministry initiative.

## Chapter 9    Ongoing youth ministry

This chapter will help you to ask:

- How are we doing?

- Are we fulfilling our mission statement?

- What do we need to do next?

# Sharing this book

'**Nobody told me this was happening**' – *a congregation member*

'**Why do they only ask us when they want money?**' – *a PCC member*

'**I don't know what to say to young people**' – *a potential yet reluctant volunteer*

'**Youth what?**'

This book is for sharing – it gives practical advice on engaging with young people by enabling the whole church to develop a ministry to and from young people. If it only stays in your hands, there are two possible outcomes:

1. the whole prospect seems too daunting on your own and nothing happens; or

2. some youth activity gets going at *your* instigation, under *your* leadership, in *your* spare time, at the expense of other aspects of *your* life, without due support and at risk to *your* spiritual sanity . . .

Throughout this book we will explore how to shape a youth ministry for your church, so we need to make sure that the *church* prepares itself for that ministry. Why not use the circulation list on page x to ensure the book reaches as many people as possible? (There are suggestions for some people who ought to read it; you will know who else to add to the list for your church.)

# Using this book

You can use this book in one of two ways – either as a text to be read by individuals and then discussed at a meeting or for an eight-week discussion and training programme.

Individuals can read the book as a background text and then discuss it at a church council or specially called meeting. Perhaps you have recently conducted a church audit and wish to address the issue of youth ministry or perhaps you have invited a youth work professional to come and talk and wish to do some preparatory reading. This book will help you think through how to develop a youth ministry and begin to answer some of the fundamental questions to get started.

Alternatively, you might want to use it as an eight-part course or discussion programme, by using the eight **session outlines** at the end of each chapter.

Each chapter offers the following:

- an **exploration** of the topic which can be used as background reading for each **session outline** as well as in its own right;

- an **evaluation tool** to help you evaluate initiatives which have arisen from your church discussion;

- a **summary**, outlining the fundamental questions to ask and necessary action to take. The **summary** also offers a selection of useful resources on each topic (see the *Bibliography* on page 99 for full details of each resource);

- A **session outline** to enable you to explore the chapter topic within your church and develop a locally appropriate strategy for your ministry.

## Session outlines

These are ready-to-use plans designed for a 90-minute meeting format. They can be used as a progressive course or independently and the timetable can be adapted to suit your church's needs. The outlines assume that all those attending have read this book as a background text to the sessions.

When offering church time for discussion about youth ministry, you may find the following practical tips helpful:

- ensure that your meeting space is conducive to discussion – for example, sitting in a circle makes people feel included and enables everyone to see and to be heard whereas for some, sitting in rows can remind them of the classroom;

- allow time fully to explore the issues raised – remember that many people will only speak once they feel confident, often only at the second or third invitation – initiating a youth ministry should not be the last item on an already over-full agenda;

- ensure that the meeting 'leader' or chair has the ability to encourage everyone to speak without allowing the meeting to be dominated by one or two louder individuals, and is able to elicit direct action and responsibility from the discussion;

- have someone take concise minutes outlining the action decided upon and circulate them promptly;

- offer refreshments at an appropriate time – drinks and snacks at the start of a specially arranged meeting can make participants feel relaxed and welcomed, a warm cup of tea after a lengthy church council discussion can make members feel valued and appreciated for their hard work.

Each **session outline** is followed by **facilitator's notes** for the person facilitating the discussion and a **group notes** page that can be photocopied for each participant.

## Evaluation

Evaluations should be a positive process – not just a list of things that 'could be better', but a chance to celebrate what is good and has worked. They need not be an over arduous process either, the eight different **evaluation tools** offer different methods for evaluating the action taken. Whilst each is directly relevant to the chapter it follows, many can be interchanged and used as you find appropriate.

It is important to share the evaluation method with those from whom you are asking responses, so that they know that what they say or write will be taken seriously and treated confidentially. Be sure to share the results of the evaluation with them too, so that they know that they have been listened to, as well as the rest of the church family – keep them involved through the church council and church newsletters as appropriate.

However you use this book, it is important to have cross-church representation. If it is left to the sub-committee of the PCC that has raised its concern for young people, or the volunteers who run the youth group, a number of things are likely to happen:

- the youth ministry is not owned by the church;

- those present feel unsupported and potentially resentful;

- other members of the congregation are unable to offer support, express concerns or ask questions;

- young people's needs become compartmentalized;

- a holistic approach to young people is not offered.

Offering the whole church the chance to play a part in the developing of the youth ministry allows them to take ownership of this part of the church's mission. Further down the line it will also prevent the responsibility for the ministry being held by one or two already over-stretched individuals.

## Summary

### The questions to ask:

- Who else should read this book?

- How can we take this forward?

### Points for action:

- complete the list on page x and share the book;

- put the proposal of an eight-part church course to your church council or education committee.

### Useful resources:

- Ridge Burns and Pam Campbell, *Create In Me A Youth Ministry*, Victor Books, Illinois, 1994

- National and Diocesan Youth Network of the Church of England, *Youth A Part*, National Society/Church House Publishing, 1996

- National and Diocesan Youth Network of the Church of England, *Youth A Part Resources Pack*, National Society/Church House Publishing, 1996

# 2 What is Youth Ministry?

## This chapter will help you:

✔ come to an understanding of what youth ministry is;

✔ build a vision of a youth ministry that is relevant and appropriate for your church;

✔ prepare to take action.

## Getting to grips with youth ministry

So far we have used the term youth 'ministry'. For many this may be a new phrase. A more familiar phrase may be youth 'work'. The reason for using the word *ministry* directly after the word *youth* is to encourage us to think of our church's relationship with young people as part of its overall ministry. The word ministry implies a comprehensive approach to young people and is also understood as a two-way process – giving ministry to and receiving ministry from young people. By virtue of the fact that you are reading this book, this concept is unlikely to phase you, but for many this could be difficult to grapple with. A traditional picture of youth ministry may be provision of activity for young people – perhaps offering a designated group at regular intervals which young people of a defined age group are invited to attend. Nothing wrong with that, but I would venture to suggest that this is only one small aspect of what youth ministry can be.

As an adult member of a congregation, I expect to participate in (help to plan, support in practical ways and benefit from) a regular act of worship that nurtures me spiritually. I know that I will not find every element of that worship to be of my exact choosing, but I will expect to come away having connected with God in a way that is appropriate to me, and having been furthered in my understanding of God's message to us through teaching that I can engage with. In addition to this regular worship, I also expect to be challenged in my Christian awareness and understanding through study with fellow Christians who are able to relate to me in my state of learning and exploration. In addition to both of these elements I also look for fellowship through the church, for opportunities to meet other members of the congregation with whom I can build appropriate relationships. Whilst I expect us all to be members of one church family and to be challenged to respond to all of its members, I also expect that there will be some members with whom I naturally form closer relationships based, for example, on our age, a common career or a similar family status. If I was a young person in the same congregation, should I expect anything different?

The concept of youth ministry is one of a holistic ministry that embraces young people's lives and facilitates them in ministering to others in the church family. For some churches the first stage in developing a youth ministry will mean moving on from the proverbial Sunday night youth group; for others it will mean finding ways of introducing the church to young people in the local area. The important thing to remember is that there is no magic formula and no one way to do things: the youth ministry in each church should be unique to that church.

## Setting aside time

Having established what youth ministry could be, the next step is to begin to prepare to move on and shape a ministry that is right for your church. This will take time and commitment, but effort spent in preparation will pay dividends later. Very often a church will feel the need to act immediately and, as a result, set up something that is unsupported and not owned by the church.

It is here that an initial church meeting is vital. Even if it is inappropriate for your church to follow the other **session outlines** offered, the initial exploration and decisions as to how to proceed require total church representation. We have identified the importance of a whole church approach to youth ministry, so it follows that the whole church should be represented in exploring the possibilities of youth ministry. Consider holding such a discussion during a designated church meeting or at an extra special church council meeting.

It is important that the meeting is offered with the intention of hearing everyone and also moving forward. There are two main reasons for this. Firstly, we must acknowledge that, in nearly all of our churches, young people are not the predominant age group so awareness of their needs may be new for many. Secondly, we should acknowledge that many congregations comprise predominantly older people who were not teenagers (and I use that term in its broadest sense to mean 11–18-year-olds) and young adults in the way that young people are now. The concept of a teenager is post-second-world-war, and for those who were in their teens before the war the transition from childhood to adulthood did not have the teenage 'grace period' we so rightly afford young people now. One can identify one's own time as a young adult as being very different from that of 18–25-year-olds today, as each generation has faced different challenges and expectations, for example in terms of Further Education or career prospects. It is natural that these differences can cause resentment and frustration from all age groups. They can also be a point for discussion and celebration, but only when sufficient time is given to their exploration and discussion. This means young people listening to, and learning from, adults' experiences and opinions – I am not promoting a one-sided learning curve here!

It may be helpful to bring in someone from outside to speak to the meeting or perhaps facilitate it. Such a person could be your denominational youth officer or a representative from a local or national youth agency. You may find it helpful to enlist the support of another church that has been through this exploratory process, provided that this is supportive for your own church development – there is a danger of seeking their answers rather than shaping your own ministry.

When setting up your meeting you may find the following tips helpful:

- ensure that there is true representation from across the church – look to see that the following groups are represented:

    children

    young people and young adults in their 20s and 30s

    adults in their 40s, 50s, 60s, 70s, 80s, 90s

    families

    parents and grandparents

    single people

    couples without children

    those working with existing children's and youth groups

    attached uniformed organizations

    new members of the congregation

    more established members of the congregation

    members from congregations of all your different services

- if any of these groups are unused to attending and speaking at church meetings, how will they be supported, encouraged to speak and listened to?

- is this a good time for the church to have this discussion and then act upon it? (Just before summer in a church where everyone disappears on holiday, for example, or before an interregnum, might not be a good time.)

- offer a comfortable meeting room with some refreshments – this can help to offer a more relaxed atmosphere, maybe even providing some comfort for what can be quite an emotive subject;

- set up the room in a format conducive to group discussion (e.g. in-the-round as opposed to lecture style);

- choose a facilitator who is able to be sympathetic to everyone's needs and enable the meeting to move on;

- circulate copies of the questions (see page 11);

- be prepared to hold a follow-up/second meeting;

- ensure that the outcomes of the meeting are shared with those who were unable to be present, e.g. through the notices, newsletter, announcement, sermons.

A suggested outline for an initial meeting, which you may find helpful, is included at the end of this chapter.

## What to discuss

In the **group notes** for this chapter there is a list of discussion questions that you may wish to use – the notes are included as a separate page so they can be photocopied and distributed to those at the meeting. During the meeting the facilitator may wish to use the accompanying notes to encourage discussion. The *Youth A Part Resources Pack* also has some excellent resources to help facilitate a discussion on youth ministry.

As you will see from the list of questions, the principal aim is to start to come to a corporate vision. The importance of having a vision at the outset is to:

- enable everyone to share in the overall picture and see where the ministry is heading;

- shape a ministry that is appropriate for your particular church;

- form a frame of reference in the building and evaluating of the youth ministry.

Such a meeting should be an exciting time and an opportunity for the church to move forward in its mission. However, be prepared for the fact that individuals may need to express concerns, doubts and fears before they can move forward. This is an important part of the developmental process and, if they are allowed to be heard, the individuals may then feel able to move forward more positively. It is impossible to predict what these concerns might be, but in my experience of working with churches, I have found three common areas of concern (throughout this book, I have used genuine examples and experiences, but have changed the names of parishes and individuals involved to respect their privacy):

1. Individuals have had a bad experience of a particular group of young people and do not have a relationship with other young people to counterbalance their concerns about young people's behaviour:

   *In one rural benefice I worked with, a group of about ten young people had been caught causing damage to shop and house windows in the village. On one evening they had broken a window in the church building, not realizing that the church verger was inside. Although he was angry to see the damage, the verger decided to go outside and talk with the young people, attempting to find out why they were behaving in this destructive way through calm, ordered discussion, feeling that confronting their behaviour with anger could just make the situation worse. When he approached the somewhat surprised young people they laughed at him and shouted abuse whilst running away from him. The verger remained hurt, shocked and very distressed.*

2. A previous attempt to run a youth group or youth activity in the church has been unsuccessful:

   *One particular town church set up a Sunday morning group for teenagers at the same time as the children's Sunday School. The group had started fairly successfully with a group of about six teenagers who were children of church families. However, finding leaders for the group was always difficult as many of the adults in the congregation felt they did not want to be out of the Sunday morning worship every week. As the group of teenagers got older and moved on, there seemed to be no natural intake of younger children, the next age group in the church families still being of Sunday School age. The two leaders who had led the group week in, week out for the past four years felt disgruntled and unsupported and took the opportunity to close the group. Sadly, there was a great sense of failure and a perceived lack of need for provision for teenagers through such a group.*

3. There is concern that developing a youth ministry will lead to a para-church organization for young people:

   *A large city church had spent some time at a Christian conference at which they had met up with a church of very similar churchmanship and geographical and socio-economic status. The church they had met had established a youth outreach programme which had successfully attracted over 200 young people and young adults from across the city. This church had a very clear vision of 'meeting young people where they are' and to that end had provided for their needs by establishing a new weekly worship meeting for this particular group, held in an alternative city centre venue with age-appropriate music, lighting and liturgy. The local church was concerned as its vision was to 'meet young people where they are and bring them gently into the life of the church'. They did not want to establish what they saw as an alternative congregation and felt too frightened to initiate any new youth ministry for fear that it would result in, to use their terms, 'para-church that did not relate to our [their] church'.*

The response to such concerns will come from the church and those at the meeting, but do be aware of the fact in any gathered group of adults, there may be a significant proportion who are not in contact with any young people.

# 'Outside in' or 'inside out'?

This is one of the most fundamental decisions in your approach to youth ministry and both options are of equal value and potential. 'Outside in' neatly captures an approach by which a church seeks to meet young people on their own territory, where they feel comfortable, and build a ministry around them. An 'inside out' approach offers the alternative, whereby a church seeks to build a ministry with the young people already connected with the church and then develop the ministry to those outside of its life. Let us take two examples:

**St Mary's** took an 'outside in' approach, feeling that there were several unreached young people on the large estate in the town. The church recruited and trained a team of outreach volunteers, who developed a social youth group in the estate's community centre. Always overt about its intentions, the programme offered social fun and an opportunity for positive relationships to develop. After eighteen months, it became appropriate for the team to offer a discussion group for the teenagers and a holiday play scheme for younger children. Soon several families were involved in the various playscheme activities and it then became appropriate for St Mary's to develop a family worship service once a month in the community centre. Several of the teenagers were involved in the service and soon need was felt for a Bible study group for them after the family services. The ministry grew on the estate and complemented the services and activities at the church itself.

**St Paul's** is a church of similar make-up which adopted an 'inside out' approach. The church recruited and trained a volunteer team to run a weekly youth group for the few teenagers involved in church life. Over a period of two years the group grew in numbers to include several young people who had previously been involved in the church as children but had subsequently left. The team began to offer a Bible

study and discussion group on another night to complement the social programme of the youth group. After six months, the discussion group felt it appropriate to reach out to those not involved in church life. Some of the young people and volunteers developed a one-day holiday club on the town's largest estate. Taking a biblical theme was a great success and the holiday club was repeated during the next school holidays, developing into a week's club in the school summer holidays. Several teenagers from the estate began to get involved and, when invited, took up the church's invitation to join its youth group. The ministry grew on the estate and the church was able to accommodate its new members.

Both examples demonstrate how a youth ministry can develop and take seriously the Bible's call for social action. However, the starting points were vastly different because the long-term goals were the opposite of one another. You will need to be very clear whether your goal is to take the church to young people or to bring young people to the church.

## Action

Having set a plan of action for your church, use the following chapters to support you in the development of your youth ministry. Don't forget to keep the church informed of the outcome of the meeting and each development as it is discussed and made.

## Evaluation

Use the following *Congregation questionnaire on youth work* as an evaluation of your church's thoughts about young people and any existing youth ministry. Bring the responses to your initial meeting as the basis for discussion.

You can use the same questionnaire to review your youth ministry after six months or a year.

# Congregation questionnaire on youth work

We are currently reviewing the work with young people and are keen to know the views of members of the congregation. Therefore, please complete as fully as possible and return

to .................................................................. by ..................................................................

1.  How many young people (aged 11–18 years) do you think are involved in the activities of this church?

2.  Do you think the church should be doing more for young people?  YES/NO
    If YES
    2a.   What should be done?

3.  Do you think young people should be more involved in the life of the church?
    YES/NO
    If YES
    3a.   In what ways would you suggest?

4.  Have you spoken to anyone between the ages of 11 and 18 years at church within the past two weeks?
    YES/NO
    If YES
    4a.   Is the young person related to you? YES/NO
    4b.   Do you speak to that young person on a regular basis? YES/NO

5.  Have you spoken to anyone between the ages of 11 and 18 years outside of church within the last two weeks? YES/NO
    If YES
    5a.   Is the young person related to you? YES/NO
    5b.   Do you speak to that young person on a regular basis? YES/NO

6.  How much does your church spend on youth work a year?
    £ ............................./ DON'T KNOW

7.  What do you think the Church/Gospel has to offer young people today?

Thank you for your help with this questionnaire.

Source: Dave Green and Peter Ball, in National and Diocesan Youth Network of the Church of England, *Youth A Part Resources Pack*

# Young people and the church

## What's happening now – survey checklist

In using this checklist remember to involve any link groups identified in discussion, so that as full a picture as possible is obtained.

As this is a document for the church's use, you need to define how, for example, you count young people, e.g. is someone who comes about once a month a regular attender?

1.  How many young people aged 11–18 years are involved in any church activity, including attending services? List the activity, when it happens and how many young people are involved.

2.  Are some young people involved in more than one activity? If yes, then note this down.

3.  Are any other youth organizations linked to the church, e.g. Scouts or Guides? Note the organization, the numbers involved, where the activity takes place, the link with the church and how strong it is.

4.  Do young people participate in any way in regular church services? Note the various ways and people involved.

5.  Are any young people elected on the PCC or any other decision-making body with the church structures? If yes, note the details and numbers.

6.  Is there any special way in which the opinions of young people are sought on a regular basis? If yes, note the details.

7.  Are young people seen as equal members of the church? If yes, note the evidence for this.

8.  In the current life of the church, what things might be offputting for young people.

10. How much money is allocated in the church budget for youth work, including training of youth workers?

11. In what ways are youth workers encouraged to receive training?

12. In what ways does the church practically and prayerfully show support to its youth leaders? Give evidence.

13. Does the church have any written, specific policy statements relating to young people and youth work? If yes, find a copy!

Source: Dave Green and Peter Ball, in National and Diocesan Youth Network of the Church of England, *Youth A Part Resources Pack*

Photocopiable

## Summary

The questions to ask:

- What is youth ministry?

- Why is it important to our church?

- What is our vision for youth ministry?

- When are we going to hold our first meeting?

## Points for action:

- Hold initial church meeting

## Useful resources:

- Steve Chalke, *The Christian Youth Manual*, Kingsway Publications, 1987

- National and Diocesan Youth Network of the Church of England, *Youth A Part*, National Society / Church House Publishing, 1996

- National and Diocesan Youth Network of the Church of England, *Youth A Part Resources Pack*, National Society / Church House Publishing, 1996

## Exploring youth ministry 1

### Session 1 outline

#### Resources needed:

- photographs of young people cut from magazines, displayed around the room;

- pens and paper for each small group;

- **group notes** copied as a handout for each person – these could be distributed prior to the meeting;

- **facilitator's notes** for the discussion facilitator;

- a copy of each **evaluation tool** from this chapter for each person;

- flipchart and pens.

#### Prayer (5 minutes)

Open with a few words of welcome and ask the group to look around them at the faces of young people. Say, 'All around us Lord, we see the faces of your young people. They look in on us at this meeting as we turn out to face them, in the desire to serve them in your name. We ask for your blessing on this meeting and for you to be with us as we take our first step forward in this most exciting of ministries, Lord. Amen.'

#### Opening activity (25 minutes: 15 minutes small groups, 10 minutes large group)

Ask the group to close their eyes and imagine their church in the year 2020. Ask, 'What changes will have taken place? What will we be focusing on? What will our priorities be? What will the church look like then? What will the congregation look like? How will young people feature in 2020?'

Divide the group into smaller groups of five or six and ask them to draw an annotated picture of their vision, detailing how young people feature in it. Ask one person in each group to be the spokesperson and bring the groups back into one large group. Ask each spokesperson to present their group's picture. Allow others to ask questions of the group.

#### Discussion (50 minutes)

For the first meeting, ask a member of the team running the session to act as 'scribe' on the flipchart. The facilitator should lead the group through the discussion questions. A suggested timing is given on the facilitator's notes, along with possibilities for small-group discussion. As the first session is an important one, you may wish to allow extra time for some questions. The group could be divided as for the opening activity.

#### Summarizing and moving on (5 minutes)

Draw the meeting to a close by summarizing the developing vision. Agree to the next step and/or next meeting as appropriate.

#### Prayer (5 minutes)

Put the pictures of the young people together on the floor or in one place on the wall and gather the group around them. Close asking for God's blessing and guidance as you take the next step in this vital ministry.

### Facilitator's notes

#### What do we understand youth ministry to be? (3 minutes)

It may be helpful to record this discussion on a flipchart or OHP in order to refer to it later when vision building.

#### Is youth ministry important to us? Why or why not? (4 minutes)

It is important to ask this question at this stage, rather than assuming everyone feels youth ministry is of equal importance. Coming to a common mind as to its importance will allow everyone to take ownership of any future ministry.

## What youth ministry is our church engaged in? (3 minutes)

Remind people of the following where appropriate:

Youth groups, outreach activity, choir, attached uniformed organizations, servers, congregation members, attendance at diocesan/regional events.

## How many young people are we in contact with? (3 minutes)

You may wish to encourage people to list these privately and add up their responses or to discuss in small groups. The purpose is to help people begin to see who it is they are talking about – moving away from an abstract concept to a realistic picture.

## Have there been any previous/are there any existing youth ministry initiatives from which we should learn? (8 minutes)

The response to this question should be given sufficient time: this is the opportunity for concerns to be shared as well as honouring and acknowledging existing youth ministry. You may wish to use small groups for discussion, with an opportunity to hear from each group.

## What is our vision for our youth ministry in our church? (8 minutes)

Encourage those present to dream and be visionary – the next question enables the group to come back to practical reality. Again small-group discussion may be helpful at this point. Use the responses to this question as the basis for your church's youth ministry Mission Statement.

## Are we an 'outside in' or an 'inside out' church? (8 minutes)

See page 10 in this chapter. A response to this question will have begun to emerge from the last question; now is the time to encourage the group to come to a decision.

## What are we going to do to enable the vision to become a reality? (8 minutes)

Allow sufficient time for specific action to be decided, then put the action into order of priority, detailing by each action: When is this going to happen? Who is going to be responsible for ensuring it happens? Who is going to form the responsible body? (Encourage those listed to fix a time to meet and get started – encourage those at the meeting to give the responsible body a clear brief.)

Be prepared for action to be as specific as the meeting dictates, for example the first action could be to have a follow-up meeting or it could be a decision to set up a youth outreach group by the end of the school term. The response will be totally dependent on your particular church and is the beginning of the shaping of your ministry.

## When are we going to review our action? (5 minutes)

This is just as important as setting the vision. Depending on what action you decide to take, you will need to set realistic review times. You will need to strike the balance between loading people down with meetings and capturing their enthusiasm, a suggestion would be to meet to review/evaluate every three months in the early stages, moving to six months and then annually (see Chapter 9: Ongoing youth ministry).

It is important to commit to evaluating the ministry before people leave the first meeting, to ensure that people feel fully engaged with the work, even if they are not going to be directly responsible for its delivery. Evaluation should not happen only occasionally or just in the early stages, but as a regular part of church life. Such a frame of reference allows the youth ministry to remain a full part of the church's life, preventing a feeling of isolation for those involved and enabling the whole congregation to feel involved with the ministry. An ongoing programme of evaluation will also promote a professional approach to youth ministry and will encourage people to get involved, seeing that they are supported by the church family.

## Exploring youth ministry 1

### Prayer

'All around us Lord, we see the faces of your young people. They look in on us at this meeting as we turn out to face them, in the desire to serve them in your name. We ask for your blessing on this meeting and for you to be with us as we take our first step forward in this most exciting of ministries, Lord. Amen.'

### Opening activity

Close your eyes and imagine your church in the year 2020.

What changes will have taken place? What will we be focusing on? What will our priorities be? What will the church look like then? What will the congregation look like? How will young people feature in 2020?

In smaller groups of five or six draw an annotated picture of your vision, detailing how young people feature in it.

Allocate a spokesperson to present your group's picture back to the larger group.

### Questions for discussion

What do we understand youth ministry to be? Is youth ministry important to us? Why or why not?

What youth ministry is our church engaged in?

How many young people are we in contact with in the church . . .

> . . . through our congregation?
> . . . in our town/village?
> . . . in our own lives?

Have there been any previous/are there any existing youth ministry initiatives from which we should learn?

What is our vision for our youth ministry in our church?

Are we an 'outside in' or an 'inside out' church?

What are we going to do to enable the vision to become a reality?

When is this going to happen?

When are we going to review our action?

### Prayer

Gather as a group around the pictures of young people and close by asking for God's blessing and guidance as you take the next step in this vital ministry.

# 3 The Team Approach

## What and why?

A team approach is, as its name suggests, an approach to youth ministry by a team of people rather than one or two isolated individuals. A common example of this kind of isolation would be:

- A lady in the congregation, Mary, has two older teenagers who have now left for university; she feels that the church failed them in some way by offering them nothing age-appropriate. Her two daughters have left home having spent the last seven

### This chapter will help you:

✔ explore and become comfortable with the concept of a team approach;

✔ build and maintain a volunteer team;

✔ understand the implications of good practice and child protection for voluntary youth work.

years disinterested in the church. Because she still has a 14-year-old daughter at home she mentions this to another parent, Anne, who agrees with her, eager that something is offered for their teenagers 'before it is too late'.

- Anne and Mary agree to take their concern to the church education committee. They prepare an excellent paper, researched with their children and some of their friends, and make their case at the next committee meeting.

- The members of the committee nod in agreement – certainly this is a most neglected age group and a great cause for concern – the researched evidence shows just how important this work is and certainly something must be done 'before it is too late'. Much discussion ensues and the decision is made to offer a weekly casual home group in term time for those aged 14+. Then the chair of the committee poses the question 'who is going to run the group?' Much shuffling and looking studiously at feet as members of the committee think through their already over-full diaries. In desperation to get something going Anne and Mary offer to start the group off and support a suitable leader once one has been found.

- Fast-forward a year and see that Anne and Mary are still the group leaders, running the group in Anne's home. Although they thoroughly enjoy being with the young people, they have struggled to find material and are currently working through a book of 20 session plans. They are on session 18 and haven't yet found suitable follow-on material. They'd really like to take some time to look through resources at the local Christian bookshop, but finding that time is hard. They fear for the group's future as Mary is starting shift work soon and Anne doesn't feel that she can keep going on her own. They are also conscious of their own children's needs and feel that, with their mums as leaders, their girls aren't able to be fully relaxed and open in the group discussions.

It probably seems obvious that any ministry of the church's should be shared amongst the church family, but just because it is obvious doesn't mean that it will always happen – so let's explore a little why youth ministry needs a team approach.

We can see how the group process model, shown in the diagram opposite, allows for all members of the church to own and participate in the youth ministry. It neatly highlights the role of the team approach and its benefits for the involvement of all. It also highlights the risk that a church must take in developing a team approach.

## Christ the role model

One of the most excellent role models is Christ himself – who didn't do it alone – he recruited a team of twelve to share the ministry. Here was the recognition that one person can't be all things to all people.

## How?

Having ascertained that a team approach is the best way forward, not least because legal guidelines (which we will explore further in a moment) show us that we should always have *at least* two leaders present when engaged in youth work, the next question is obviously how we put the theory into practice. There are three key-words for effecting a team approach: recruiting, training and maintaining.

## Recruiting

This is the perennial question of churches: 'Yes we know we need to explore the needs of our young people, but who is going to do it?' The answer has to be a serious and committed recruitment drive for a dedicated team. This applies whether you are seeking a team to take up the issues raised at the initial church meeting, as discussed in Chapter 2, or to execute some youth ministry activities you have decided to offer. A good maxim is that people don't know there is a need for help unless they are told and they don't think they have the skills unless it is pointed out to them, so I would suggest both widespread general advertising and more specific headhunting.

Advertise anywhere and everywhere! Encourage other voices to make the request, not just those commonly associated with young people. Ask the young people themselves to write notices, posters, speak in services and church gatherings. Get the word out!

# Three youth ministry models

### Military model

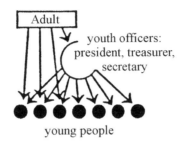

### Representative model

### Group process model

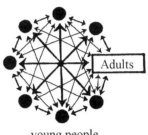

## Military model

### Good news
Faster, easier operation for adult leader. The buck stops with one person. The young people know who's boss. A strong leader may quickly attract new members. Easy for young people to drop in and out of group without worry of responsibility. Works well for businesses and the military.

### Bad news
The whole ministry depends on the strengths (and weaknesses) of one or more adult leaders. When strong leader leaves, youth ministry frequently collapses. Young people are denied the opportunity to learn responsibility, leadership, organization. No youth ownership. Adult/s often does/do all the legwork.

## Representative model

### Good news
Involves some young people in leadership. More democratic. Gives youth more visibility. Good elected officers can carry much of the load. Lets young people sample the representative form of government. Works well for national and state governments.

### Bad news
Youth officers may be elected by popularity. Those not elected may have hard feelings. Only a few young people given a chance to lead. May burn-out offficers. Adult often does everything anyway, making youth officers figure-heads. Little or no youth ownership. Occasional confusion about who's really in charge.

## Group process model

### Good news
Youth take ownership, learn res-ponsibility and leadership, and grow in self-confidence. Work shared by many. More continuity. More youth visibility. Full youth involvement possible. Works well in friendships and in youth ministry.

### Bad news
Often a greater chance for failure of some activities and programmes. Adults may get congregation's blame for failures. May be slower, more cumbersome. Requires new skills from adults. 'Star-oriented" youth workers may feel frustrated.

Source: Thom and Joani Schultz, *Kids Taking Charge*

Be clear, though, about what you are asking of volunteers. Very often people won't come forward because the task either looks too big or has no defined boundaries. Offer a clear contract – ask for volunteers to join the team for one night a week for two years, for example. People rarely come forward for jobs they perceive to be for life! A contract should contain the following elements:

● a trial period of volunteering, say three months, after which both the body inviting the volunteer and the volunteer can review their involvement and decide whether or not it is appropriate to stay;

● a defined period of service – say once a month for three terms or weekly for a year;

● any work with young people will be subject to appropriate screening (see below);

● ongoing training and support.

Include the details of such a contract in advertising and, perhaps, ask a volunteer to write about their experience. Request volunteer help for one-off events too. This is often a great way in for newcomers to youth ministry.

A general advertising sweep can be followed up by approaching individuals – headhunting if you like. I would suggest putting such a request in writing, outlining your specific requests as detailed above. Receiving a request in this way allows the recipient fully to consider their response. Giving a time when you will ring to discuss the request further can also be helpful both to the recipient and the person making the request.

# Child protection and good practice

At this point it is important to highlight the implications of good practice guidelines. Much of good practice is common sense, but it is a sensitive area, not least because of the jargon involved and the emotional issues around incidents of bad

practice. Time needs to be given to allow people to explore these issues. Here I would recommend that you seek the help of a professional to explore good practice with your church – most Church of England dioceses have a Bishop's Representative in Child Protection, each major denomination has a policy on good practice and denominational youth officers will be able to give you access to the relevant policy and either come and offer advice on good practice to your church or refer you to the most appropriate person in your area.

It is really important to try to look on child protection and good practice as a positive thing. The understanding of current good practice came about following the Children Act 1989, which states legal requirements in statutory provision for children under the age of eight. In 1993 the Home Office published *Safe From Harm,* which was a code of practice for voluntary organizations that took the law as outlined in the Children Act as a sound basis for all work with young people. *Safe From Harm* summarizes the 13 recommendations of the Children Act and gives comprehensive guidelines for voluntary organizations on managing your organization, managing and recruiting volunteers, including the screening of the adult leaders, and dealing with disclosure of abuse. Whilst it is a code of practice and not legally enforceable, *Safe From Harm* is widely respected as containing the essential guidelines for appropriate youth work which, if followed, would offer the young people and the adult leaders in the organization maximum protection against inadvertent bad practice and in the instance of an allegation of malpractice being made. *Safe From Harm* offers an accountability for those working with young people and is ignored at a church's peril! The *Safe From Harm* Summary of Recommendations is given in Appendix 1.

# Screening

Whenever a request is made for team members it must be stressed that this is subject to appropriate screening. This word leaves many cold but it is so very important that it is worth spending time as a church exploring the issues and getting to grips with its role. In the statutory sector, screening of adults means a police check, or equivalent, to ensure that adults are not able to work with minors where the adult has been convicted of certain types of offence, particularly those against young people. You may have noticed job advertisements for work with young people as often being exempt from the Rehabilitation of Offenders Act 1974.

It is advised that churches ask workers to sign a declaration that they have had no such conviction. Such a form will be available from your denominational youth officer and should be included in your denominational policy on child-protection. Take time both to explore the practical implications of such screening – seek advice as to who should issue such declaration forms, who should keep the returned copies etc. – and also the emotions around this subject. People are likely to want to explore the conflict of protection against forgiveness or the reality of such activity. Don't be afraid to make the process known publicly – taking due care of our children is a positive, professional approach to youth ministry which will encourage parents, not deter them.

It is in this matter perhaps more than any other that it is worth seeking the advice and support of a skilled professional in the area of good practice and child protection who can support you and give you direct information on matters of good practice as it pertains to your work with young people. A skilled facilitator can offer your church the opportunity to take in the necessary information, explore its implications, allow time for emotional response and then move the church on to its practical application.

## Who?

When seeking volunteers it is easy to feel desperate for help and involve anyone who expresses even the vaguest interest in youth ministry. Whilst it is important to use everyone's gifts to their fullest advantage within a Christian community, the gifts and qualities required in a youth ministry team can be simplified as follows:

- a living faith;
- respect for young people;
- a willingness to grow and learn;
- a desire to serve;
- the ability to have fun;
- patience;
- a sense of humour;
- of any age, gender or background.

You will no doubt wish to add your own to this list. Personalities that may find it hardest to be part of a youth ministry can, perhaps, be summed up as follows:

- needing to be the centre of attention;
- wishing to be a teenager – wanting to relive their youth;
- seeking a social life;
- seeking romance;
- needing to control;
- wishing to rescue all young people from the 'evils of the world';
- using youth ministry as a denial for recovery or counselling.

Consider the qualities you are looking for before you advertise for help. People fall off their chairs with laughter when I suggest the concept of interviewing potential volunteers before involving them in the youth ministry – as if they should have such a luxury! But such growth does happen in even the smallest of churches, it can be a realistic long-term goal and is promoted in *Safe From Harm*.

# Training

Training is not always just the receiving of information. Whilst there is scope for a session led by an expert in a particular area, a training session for volunteers can also be the chance for volunteers to explore a particularly relevant issue, test out some new material or share the church's vision for youth ministry. In short, it is an interactive process of sharing and learning. It should also be a time for community building and affirmation amongst the team. Any training should have as its purpose bringing the team together and moving the team on. Here again, why not consult your denominational youth officer to develop a programme of training for your church? There are many prepared materials, including *Spectrum* which is an inter-denominational training programme for volunteers. Many local authorities offer part-time or volunteer youth worker training courses too. It is always worth networking with others involved in youth work, even in a different context. Such opportunities can offer moral support, a sense of solidarity and a wealth of new resources.

Remember that a volunteer team will be a fluid body – as new people join, early basic sessions will need to be repeated. Revisiting such subjects has benefits of its own for even the most veteran of team members.

An initial training session could perhaps look at the role of the adult in youth ministry and contain discussion on the following areas:

- participation;
- group process;
- when to lead/when to follow;
- sharing fears and excitements;
- planning and executing activities;
- called to be a role model.

Include time for community building through games, fun activities or social time and offer refreshments or even a meal in the session. Follow-up sessions could include an exploration of the concept of youth ministry and the development of a mission statement for your church team or practical sessions on listening skills, appropriate behaviour, using resources, detached youth work or using prayer with young people. Consider a potential programme for the first year and consult amongst the team as to the frequency of training sessions and future subjects for exploration.

# Maintaining

Having established a team, the last thing a youth ministry needs is for it to disband out of frustration or a sense of loss of purpose. Maintenance of volunteers is an area of weakness for most churches simply due to a lack of time and an overstretched agenda. However, we all know how important it is to be valued and to feel that our precious time is being spent constructively and valuably. Maintenance of a volunteer team can fall between areas of responsibility – a church with a full-time youth minister could reasonably expect the youth minister to take ownership of this if clearly spelt out in his/her job description from the start. In a church where the youth ministry is steered completely by volunteers then a responsible body needs to take on this role from the outset. When your church is exploring how to establish a youth ministry and appointing responsibility to a particular body, perhaps a newly formed management team or an existing sub-committee of the church council, it is important to outline this area of work along with the recruiting of the volunteers.

Minimizing frustration for our precious volunteers is paramount in volunteering for any part of the church's ministry. We can all be driven mad by the following:

- meetings at which we sit about and do nothing;
- when a youth minister/leader/priest will not delegate;
- when a youth minister/leader/priest delegates but doesn't let go;

- when the youth minister/leader/priest takes credit for your hard work;

- having no training and not knowing what to do;

- feeling unappreciated or taken for granted;

- being called less than twelve hours before a meeting or event to run or prepare an activity;

- feeling that your time is not respected, e.g. being the only one to turn up for a meeting;

- poor communication and no chain of command;

- inconsistency.

To avoid these frustrations and burn-out amongst our volunteer team, the responsible body must think carefully how it can offer maintenance to the volunteers. We have talked about ongoing training and the need for social time, which can serve as a way of saying thank you. If your church appoints a responsible body in the form of a committee, then why not invite the volunteers along to regular meetings to ensure that they are both thanked and heard?

In many situations it can be appropriate to offer volunteers ongoing evaluation sessions where the volunteer has a chance to discuss their involvement and receive supportive, constructive feedback. This is easier to develop with a full-time youth minister or where a staff member has been given oversight of the volunteer team, but an evaluation process could take place in a group setting as well as at a one-to-one meeting. Why not use the **evaluation tool** in this chapter, the *Volunteer team evaluation* questionaire, which

could be either used as it stands or adapted to suit your particular situation?

One of the key reasons for the frustrations listed above is a feeling of distrust and disrespect. This can happen when a volunteer feels overridden: an example might be when the church council make a decision to run all-age confirmation groups without consulting those who run the current teenage group. Hopefully the team approach that we have talked about throughout this book will avoid such situations, but careful monitoring of decision-making and its impact on volunteers can be achieved by regular consultation with the volunteer team. Similarly, a volunteer may feel disrespected if they have been asked to get involved with the youth ministry for an initial period of a year and after 18 months no-one has discussed their ongoing involvement, taking it for granted that the volunteer will wish to remain involved.

## Evaluation

Use the following **evaluation tool** to support your volunteer team. This can be adapted for use in either a group setting or a one-to-one meeting. Its purpose is to offer volunteers a chance to express concerns and feelings about their role in the youth ministry and for the church to affirm and thank them for their work. Ensure that the setting for the evaluation meeting is conducive to discussion, offer refreshments and allow sufficient time for everyone to contribute fully. You may like to copy the questions for volunteers to enable them to prepare and make notes on what they want to say before the meeting.

## Evaluation questionnaire

## Volunteer team evaluation

Please answer the following questions:

1. Complete in your own words: 'This ministry position has been satisfying for me because . . .'

   ..............................................................................................................................

2. 'The major frustrations in this ministry position have been . . .'

   ..............................................................................................................................

3. Which skills have you been called upon to use in your youth ministry?

   ..............................................................................................................................

4. Do you feel you have received sufficient support in your ministry position?  Yes/No

   What support have you welcomed? What other support can we offer you?

   ..............................................................................................................................

   ..............................................................................................................................

5. Do you feel you have received sufficient training in your ministry position?  Yes/No

   What training have you welcomed?  What other training can we offer you?

   ..............................................................................................................................

   ..............................................................................................................................

6. 'I have found the following resources helpful . . .'

   ..............................................................................................................................

7. 'I would have been able to do this ministry better if . . .'

   ..............................................................................................................................

8. 'The highlights of this ministry position for me have been . . .'

   ..............................................................................................................................

9. 'A person following me in this position needs to know . . .'

   ..............................................................................................................................

10. Is there anything else you would like to discuss?

    ..............................................................................................................................

    ..............................................................................................................................

## Summary

### The questions to ask:

- Why is a team approach important?

- How is our team to be successfully developed and maintained? Who will take responsibility for this?

- How do we respond to the implications of good practice guidelines?

- What qualities of leadership are we looking for in our volunteer team?

### Points for action:

- read *Safe From Harm*;

- involve a professional in the field of good practice to explore the practical implications with your church;

- carry out action arising from this meeting;

- hold a second meeting using the following **session outline**;

- appoint a responsible body to undertake the recruiting, training and maintaining of the volunteer team.

### Useful resources:

- J. Dunn, *The Effective Leader,* Kingsway Publications, 1995

- NCEC, *Spectrum*, NCEC, 1996

- David R. Smith, *Safe From Harm*, Home Office, London, 1993

- Your denominational Youth Officer and Child Protection Officer

- *Policy on Child Protection: Policy Statement by the House of Bishops of the General Synod of the Church of England and Recommendations as to its Implementation*, Church House Publishing, 1999 (NB most dioceses have issued a Diocesan Policy Statement and each major denomination has an equivalent child protection policy)

- Your local authority Youth and Community Service

## Exploring youth ministry 2

## Session 2 outline

### Resources needed:

- a roll of masking tape;

- a Bible with passages marked;

- a copy of the *Three Youth Ministry Models* for everyone to see (see page 19);

- flipchart and pens;

- **group notes** copied as a handout for each person – these could be distributed prior to the meeting;

- **facilitator's notes** for the discussion facilitator;

- a copy of the **evaluation tool** for each person;

- a copy of the summary of *Safe From Harm* recommendations, Appendix 1, for each person;

- list of positive leadership qualities and undesirable qualities from the section *Who?* earlier in this chapter on page 21.

### Prayer (5 minutes)

Read aloud Ephesians 4.1-13, allowing time for silent reflection. Ask for God's blessing and guidance on the session.

## Opening activity (10 minutes)

Move the chairs to one side and tape a line of masking tape across the middle of the meeting area. Explain to the group that they have to work together as one body to cross the line; if they do not, they will fall into the deadly swamp that the line is hiding and be eaten alive! Tell them that you will give them a certain number of body parts which can touch the ground and that these are collective for the group. These must be the only parts touching the ground as the group crosses the line. Each person in the group must be touching at least one other person in some way. So, for example, if you have ten people in the group, you might allow them to have ten feet touching the ground and two hands. One way that they could achieve this would be for eight people to hop and one person to walk pushing the final person as a wheelbarrow on their hands. Offer body parts appropriate to the number and ability of your group. Accommodate their needs, for example if you have a wheelchair user, include two wheels in the collective parts. The aim of this game is for the group to begin to work as a team. You must not interfere. Repeat once or twice as time allows.

## Discussion (60 minutes)

Ask someone in the group to act as 'scribe' if you feel it is appropriate.

The facilitator should lead the group through the discussion questions. A suggested timing is given which can be adapted to suit your church's needs. If you have invited an outside speaker to talk about child protection and good practice, you will need to adjust your meeting accordingly.

## Summarizing and moving on (10 minutes)

Go through the discussion notes with the large group. Assign any action to be taken to members of the group and detail the deadline for completing the action. Ask for group consensus on the action list and note who will be responsible for distributing the lists and by when. Confirm arrangements for the next session.

## Prayer (5 minutes)

Read aloud 1 Corinthians.12-27. Give thanks for being part of a body and for the contributing each of the 'parts' has made to this group.

## Facilitator's notes

### What do we understand by a 'team approach'? (5 minutes)

Ensure that everyone is on common ground by asking this question, list key words and phrases on the flipchart.

### Is it one we should adopt? Why? (8 minutes)

It is important for the group to come to an agreement on this. Although it is likely that they will wish to adopt a team approach it cannot be assumed and time must be given to allow people to voice concerns and queries.

### Which model of youth ministry do we see as appropriate for our church? (6 minutes)

Look at the diagram *Three Youth Ministry Models* on page 19 and allow time for exploration.

### What qualities do we consider to be important in leadership? (8 minutes)

Put up the list of positive leadership qualities and undesirable qualities from page 21 on the flipchart now. Allow time for clarification and additions from the group. Allow time further to explore the non-desirable qualities.

### How are we going to recruit, train and maintain a volunteer team? Who is going to be the responsible body? (10 minutes)

Ensure that realistic steps are outlined and that a responsible body is outlined.

## How do good practice guidelines impact our work? (8 minutes)

Be very disciplined with the group and make sure that the practical implications are listed, before moving on to the emotional response to good practice.

## How do we respond to good practice in youth ministry? (15 minutes)

Allow time for an emotive response to the issue of good practice. People may find the need for such analysis of their work and possible change upsetting or frightening. They may also be worried about the prospect of an increased workload. Time needs to be given for such feelings to be shared. Close this question by reminding each other that these are pro-active steps to take and a positive action on behalf of our young people.

## Exploring youth ministry 2

### Prayer

Listen to Ephesians 4.1-13, followed by time for silent reflection. Ask for God's blessing and guidance on the session.

### Opening activity

As a group you will be asked to work together as one body to cross the line; if you do not, you will fall into the deadly swamp that the line is hiding and be eaten alive! You will be given a certain number of body parts which can touch the ground and told that these are collective for the group. These must be the only parts touching the ground as the group crosses the line. Each person in the group must be touching at least one other person in some way.

### Questions for discussion

What do we understand by a 'team approach'?

Is it one we should adopt? Why?

Which model of youth ministry do we see as appropriate for our church?

What qualities do we consider to be important in leadership?

How are we going to recruit, train and maintain a volunteer team? Who are going to be the responsible body?

How do good practice guidelines impact our work?

How do we respond to good practice in youth ministry?

### Prayer

Listen to 1 Corinthians 12-27. Give thanks for being part of a body and for the contribution each of the 'parts' has made to this group.

# Relational Ministry

## What?

We can easily take Jesus Christ's lead in holding relationships as the central force of ministry. Dr Roland Martinson, writer on youth ministry, says:

For young people in early and late adolescence, faith is primarily a person. It's incarnate in a relationship, and I think that's fitting. Jesus Christ was God become incarnate for us so we can see and taste and hear and pick up on what God does when God becomes a human being. What a volunteer does for a teenager is to demonstrate some of what faith looks like in living flesh.

### This chapter will help you:

✔ begin to explore the concept of relational ministry;

✔ build a strategic approach to developing relationships;

✔ revisit basic listening skills;

✔ consider how to develop appropriate, healthy relationships.

For a young person, good relationships with other adults can offer them a chance to receive a balanced perspective by hearing from a wider variety of people, discuss issues facing them that, perhaps, they can't share with their family members and help them experience positive relationships as they develop new friends and make major life decisions.

Relational ministry is about building positive relationships. This applies to young people, fellow leaders and the Church. Ensure that the positive, appropriate relationships that are explored here are modelled with others in the leadership team and the Church. Being a good relationship builder is a quality that is difficult to teach, but there is room for training on listening skills, appropriate relationships and exploration as to how to build good relationships.

It is easy to become bound up in the 'doing' of youth ministry, perhaps running the youth group or persuading the church council for more funds. Relational ministry is hard because it is less tangible than such activity, but it is the essence of Christianity. Establishing relationships is identification with people in a real way in the sense that Christ 'The Word became flesh and dwelt among them'.

> Accompanying is essentially an attitude and a skill which is rooted in the humanity of the accompanist, where the chief quality is the ability to 'be' alongside the accompanied . . . For a Christian accompanying can be seen as a reflection of God's nature, and is compassionate, loving and grounded in the concept of free will. (Maxine Green and Chandu Christian, 'The art of accompanying', *Accompanying*, Church House Publishing, 1998)

# How?

Developing relationships is hard work and does need a strategic approach. We have already talked about consulting the young people as to their vision of a youth ministry and such consultancy can be maintained through positive relationships. We need to make time for relationships to develop, perhaps through organized activity – home groups, social events or church projects. Often churches like to balance a large youth group with small house groups in which young people are afforded the chance to talk more intimately. If you do offer a large youth group or gathering, structure in some social time for the members to chat informally, though be careful that individuals aren't left without someone to talk to and ensure that this time offers the chance for those leading the group to engage in socializing. Often there is so much to do to get the next

part of the session ready that there is no time to be alongside the young people.

We also need to meet young people outside the church setting; church is an option today and we must care enough to go to young people, not expecting them to come to us. It may be appropriate for your church to establish a dedicated outreach programme for young people or to ensure that an existing programme includes opportunities for young people to invite their non-involved friends. A recent survey in America as to why people become part of a Christian Community found the following responses:

- through crusades                                  0.1%
- through church programmes              4%
- through clergy/by walking in              4%
- through church visitations/
  door-to-door calling                              1%
- through the invitation of a friend  70-90%

The following suggestions offer practical pointers for developing and maintaining relationships:

- pray for the people involved;
- ask God for a sincere interest in young people;
- be casual, don't work too hard at being friendly unless it is natural for you;
- practice the discipline of learning names – use whatever system will help you;
- do not force your way into situations where you know you will be unwelcome;
- be yourself – don't try to impress with excessive humour or overdone antics. You don't have to be a comedian, athlete or clown to love a young person;
- ask open questions (i.e. ones that don't require just a yes or no answer) and don't be afraid to be educated;
- be adaptable and expect to change pace from time to time;
- keep a close personal record of significant relationships, a diary is of great value, especially in prayer;

- keep a communication record to ensure that you are aware of significant dates and events in the young people's lives. Such a record also helps you to see if there are young people with whom you haven't recently been in contact (some examples of communication records appear later in this chapter);

- remember we need to earn the right to each relationship;

- regularly bring in outside leaders to run the youth group (e.g. a drama group to lead a workshop, a local professional to talk about their work or a youth worker from another church) to allow those normally 'up front' to be alongside the young people;

- consider allocating responsibility for 'checking in' with the young people across the volunteer team, so that each adult ensures that, say, five young people receive regular affirmation, conversation and support;

- offer a regular time when the adult leader is available for a chat, although this will be in confidence, ensure that good practice guidelines are followed and never allow one leader to be alone with a young person. One youth minister I know is in McDonalds on two afternoons after school and available to chat, this offers her the protection of a public place and offers the young people the chance to see if she is available without walking in on someone else's conversation;

- consider a basic listening skills course for all involved – young people and adults alike;

- offer regular, unconditional affirmation.

The basic principles of starting a conversation are outlined in the following box. You may wish to develop this into a training session on listening skills as indicated above, particularly with regard to the issue of confidentiality and reporting abuse. Your denominational youth officer will be able to help with this particular area.

## Guidelines for starting conversations:

1. Introduce yourself first, if this is the first meeting.

2. Open conversation with a topic that may be of interest to both of you, or with a non-threatening question or by talking together about an object, piece of jewellery or clothing the other has on.

3. Ask informational questions that will provide 'free information' on which the conversation may be built. Informational questions may lead to a subject of interest to both of you. For example; 'Have you lived in other places?', 'Have you travelled outside the country?', 'Where did you go on holiday?'

4. Look at the person, make eye contact while not doing something else at the same time.

5. Show you are listening by following a comment with a further question or comment relating to what the person just said.

6. Return comments about yourself without the other person having to ask. Avoid an interview type of situation and develop a sharing relationship.

7. Avoid asking questions that result in either a yes or no answer.

8. Smile occasionally, but don't always laugh or giggle.

9. Use questions and a tone of voice that convey sincerity and do not sound phoney.

10. Do not probe into personal areas unless the speaker has volunteered the information.

11. Allow silences to occur when the other person is considering what to answer, or when both of you are thinking of new directions to take the conversation.

Source: Dr B. Varenhorst and Lee Sparks, *Training Teenagers for Peer Ministry*

Photocopiable

## Inappropriate relationships

When we refuse to take young people seriously, we adults lose out and get accused of practising tokenism. What is worse, young people become full of apathy. Unfortunately we see the cause of it lying within young people rather than seeing our contribution in creating it. (Maxine Green and Chandu Christian, 'The art of accompanying', *Accompanying*, Church House Publishing, 1998)

People get involved in youth ministry for a number of reasons and, sadly, it is inevitable that some of these reasons are inappropriate in relationships with young people. Obviously there are people whose motives are those of abuse, which is completely intolerable, and we have looked in Chapter 3 at ways of preventing abusive adults getting involved in youth ministry. There are also adults whose reason for getting involved may be social, egotistical, a wish to fill an emotional void in their own lives, or to seek recognition, or out of a desire to parent young people they see as disaffected. At this point we need to recognize that almost all of us will identify with some of these needs to some extent, but it is important to identify the false promises that we can make and the myths that we perpetrate by fulfilling unhealthy relationships. Let us take three examples:

# Inappropriate relationships

| Role: | You are my child, I am your parent | You are my friend, I am your peer | You are my anything, I am your everything |
|---|---|---|---|
| Myth: | Your parents are inadequate | Your friends aren't good enough | I can do it all and do it all the time |
| Promise: | I can be a better parent to you | I can be your best friend | I have it all and will give it all if you do it my way |
| Adult's need: | makes him/her popular | makes him/her feel liked and accepted | puts him/her in control |
| Effect on young person: | look at the adult to meet their needs rather than their parents | look to the adult to meet their needs at the expense of their friends – can cause resentment within their peer group | exploits them by using the young person's desire to be accepted |

Source: Dana A. Max, *Right Roles and Relationships in Youth Ministry*

Photocopiable

Obviously these are extreme examples, but it is easy to see how we can build an unhealthy relationship without intent. Young people who are in need often give themselves up to be what the youth leader wants them to be. Seeing this influence take place and experiencing the feelings of acceptance that this offers is, obviously, flattering but it is also inappropriate. Surely an adult's duty in a youth ministry relationship is to facilitate the young person in discerning what the Holy Spirit wants them to be? The Trinity offers God as the parent, Jesus as the friend and the Holy Spirit as the gift-giver through the young person's relationships and it is important for the adult leader to recognize and personally know this.

## Being a friend, being a role model

An important consideration at this stage is to think through the potential impact positive adult relationships can have on a young person. Whilst we have acknowledged the importance of positive, appropriate relationships between adults and young people, we need to define to what extent this constitutes a friendship. A friendship is usually thought of as a two-way relationship of affection, trust, support, give and take and 'being there for one another'. It is perhaps worth exploring to what extent an appropriate relationship can be maintained between an adult leader and a young person if such a friendship exists. By this I mean that, whilst it is important for the adult in the relationship to be open, honest and true to themselves, it is perhaps unfair to expect the young person fully to be able to offer support and consistency in the way one might demand of a friend. Whilst the young person may be fully able to do so, a *dependency* on the young person to fulfil this role can be unfair. The young person needs to have the freedom to explore and make mistakes within the friendship. For the adult facing a particular personal issue, they need to be able to accept all the support and help the young person offers without coming to rely on that

young person to fulfil their social and emotional needs. Friendship from a young person should be accepted and acknowledged but never relied upon to the exclusion of other adult friendship. Friendship to a young person similarly should not attempt to replace other young people. This sentiment may initially cause concern amongst those involved in young people's lives and I offer it as a point for discussion.

I would also urge those involved in youth ministry to consider to what extent adults are called to be role models. One's very involvement causes one to become something of a role model and it goes without saying that we must be as positive a role model as possible. However, we should ask ourselves whether this means we need to be fully up to date in terms of current music trends, fashion, television etc. Obviously for some adults this will naturally happen as they have a personal interest in these areas, but is it necessary, or indeed appropriate, to feign an interest in an area of music in which one has no interest? I would argue that the role of the adult is to be true to themselves, and if this means contributing to a conversation by simply listening because the adult in question isn't aware, say, of the latest television trend, then that is the most honest and positive contribution to make. Is it not more empowering for a young person to be able to share something of their experience with someone who is willing to listen *and* learn? Is it the duty of adults fully to enter the world of the young person? Is it not offensive to the young person to attempt to be untrue to ourselves? These are decisions you will need to come to in your own ministry.

## Sharing personal information

The other area to explore is that of appropriate sharing. An example of sharing a personal experience happened to James and Clare, youth ministers in Georgia, USA:

> *James was employed by the church as their youth minister and Clare, his wife, supported him in his*

*full-time ministry. The Bible study group had chosen to look at human relationships and James and Clare decided that they would share their personal story. The group met and James and Clare told them all about how they had both had previous sexual relationships before they met one another. They talked openly and honestly about how this had affected their marriage, their feelings of jealousy and guilt and their sadness and repentance at the situation. The young people listened more intently than ever and thanked them for being so open and honest with them. They told James and Clare that no-one had ever been that honest with them before and, whilst James and Clare felt extremely vulnerable and exhausted, they also felt that they had done an important thing in offering the young people a real life experience. They hoped that by sharing their difficulties from their experience the young people could use that information when faced with similar decisions themselves.*

On the other hand, Elaine, a single youth minister in South Yorkshire, was engaged to be married to Greg.

*The young people in the church knew Greg and when he visited Elaine he got involved in her work. At a house group one evening the topic for discussion was sexual relationships and one young woman, Jane, asked Elaine if she had 'slept with Greg'. Elaine responded by gently asking Jane why she needed to know and what answer she would like to hear. Jane thought about it for a moment and responded that, actually, she would rather not know because if Elaine said yes she had slept with Greg then Jane felt she would think 'Oh well then it's alright for me, I mean they've done it and still survived', but if Elaine answered that she hadn't slept with Greg, Jane would feel 'guilty that I have been sleeping with my boyfriend and want to stop, but I can't talk to you about it Elaine because you don't understand'. Elaine then felt able to respond to Jane's needs and talk with her about her situation without Jane being influenced by Elaine's decisions*

*before her. Elaine hoped that the ensuing group discussion empowered the young people to make their own decisions without the influence of her experience or her telling them what to do and also felt that she had managed to maintain a little personal privacy.*

These two examples show how adults can make different responses. Again it is a personal choice of the adult involved as to how much personal information they wish to share and whether they feel that they can handle the young person's reaction to that information.

# Evaluation

Distribute the 'Guidelines for starting conversations' listed on page 31 to those involved in relational youth ministry.

Ask individuals to consider one significant conversation they have recently held with a young person and to mentally 'grade' themselves as to how they fulfilled each guideline. Ask them to consider whether they feel they used any of the guidelines, how well they did, whether they were aware of how they were listening, etc. Assure them that this is a private exercise and not a test!

In a gathered group (perhaps before a volunteer training session exploring listening skills) break into small groups and encourage the groups to explore their responses to each guideline, whether they consider other guidelines should be added, where they feel they need further training and support.

As a large group feed back and ensure that identified training needs can be met. Consider developing an extended list of guidelines for your church, write up additions on a flipchart, copy and distribute in the church. You could also consider using the communication records which follow

# Communications log

| Date | Name | Phone | Subject and response | Follow-up needed | By when |
|------|------|-------|----------------------|------------------|---------|
|      |      |       |                      |                  |         |

# Communication record

Date:                                    Time:

Type of communication:

Contact initiated by:

Content of conversation:

**Action agreed on**

By young person:

By me:

Notes/other information:

# Youth contact documentation sheet

Name of leader:

Phone:

Name of young person:

Phone:

Were parents notified of meeting?

Date of meeting:

Time & duration of meeting:

Where meeting was held:

Content of meeting:
(i.e. basketball/shopping/errands/meal/etc.)

Notes/other information:

## Summary

### The questions to ask:

- How do we develop relationships with:
  - young people
  - adult leaders
  - between the youth ministry and the rest of the church?
- How can we maintain appropriate relationships?
- To what extent are we called to be
  - role models
  - friends?
- How do we evaluate our relational ministry?
- What training and support do we need?

### Points for action:

- hold third meeting using the following session outline;
- develop and maintain a good communication record;
- develop and maintain a listeners' local directory;
- organize a basic listening skills training session.

### Useful resources:

- K. Jacobs, *Swift To Hear*, SPCK, 1985
- Pete Ward, *Relational Youth Work*, Lynx Communications, 1995
- Maxine Green and Chandu Christian, *Accompanying*, Church House Publishing, 1998

## Exploring youth ministry 3

## Session 3 outline

### Resources needed:

- a piece of paper and a pen for each person;
- a copy of the *Guidelines for starting conversations* for each person (see page 31) to use as evaluation tool;
- a copy of the *Inappropriate relationships* box for each person (see page 32);
- **group notes** copied as a handout for each person – these could be distributed prior to the meeting;
- **facilitator's notes** for the discussion facilitator;
- a copy of *Just walk with me* (see page 41) for each person.

### Prayer (5 minutes)

Gather the group together in silence and say, 'Lord God, you gave us the ultimate example of relational ministry in and through the gift of your Son Jesus Christ. Be with us, we pray, as we gather to explore relational ministry and in all of our relationships. Amen.'

### Opening activity (10 minutes)

Give each person a piece of paper and a pen. Ask them to imagine that they are to be stranded on a desert island. Much like the radio programme, they are allowed to take certain things with them. However, these must be certain qualities they would like to find in the one other person who is going to be stranded with them. Ask them to list the ten qualities they would most like that person to have. Remember they do not know how long they might have to spend with that person.

Divide them into smaller groups and ask them to share their list. Ask each group to come up with a joint list of the ten most important qualities.

Ask the groups to join so that you now have two roughly equal larger groups. Ask the groups to share their lists and now come up with the three most important qualities they would like to find in that person.

Finally, bring the groups back to one large group and ask them to share their two lists. Ask these then to come up with *one* quality which they believe to be the most important of all – what would be the one quality they would most hope for? The aims of this exercise are to get people in the group working together and also to consider the qualities needed in relational ministry.

## Discussion (60 minutes)

Ask someone in the group to act as 'scribe' if you feel it is appropriate.

The facilitator should lead the group through the discussion questions. A suggested timing is given which can be adapted to suit your church's needs.

## Summarizing and moving on (10 minutes)

Go through the discussion notes with the large group. Assign any action to be taken to members of the group and detail the deadline for completing the action. Ask for group consensus on the action list and note who will be responsible for distributing the lists and by when. Confirm arrangements for the next session.

## Prayer (5 minutes)

Hand out the *Just walk with me* sheets (page 41). Read aloud and allow a few moments for personal, silent reflection.

## Facilitator's notes

### What do we understand by relational ministry? (5 minutes)

Ensure that everyone is on common ground by asking this question, list key words and phrases on the flipchart.

### Why is it important to us? (8 minutes)

It is important for the group to come to an agreement on this. It cannot be assumed and time must be given to allow people to voice concerns and queries.

### What is our strategic approach to its development in our church? (10 minutes)

Make sure that the group is really specific and direct action steps are listed.

### What are the basic skills needed to build relational ministry? (8 minutes)

Hand out the *Guidelines for starting conversations* sheets. Allow time for clarification and additions from the group. Ask the group if members would like to organize a further session on revisiting basic listening skills.

### How do we develop positive, healthy, appropriate relationships with young people? (15 minutes)

Hand out the *Inappropriate relationships* sheets. Allow time for clarification from the group. Allow time for reactions to the concept of inappropriate relationships. This continues from good practice implications for many people.

### To what extent are we called to be friends and/or to be role models? (16 minutes)

Allow time for a full and conclusive discussion.

## Exploring youth ministry 3

### Prayer

'Lord God, you gave us the ultimate example of relational ministry in and through the gift of your Son Jesus Christ. Be with us, we pray, as we gather to explore relational ministry and in all of our relationships. Amen.'

### Opening activity

You will be given a piece of paper and a pen. Imagine that you are to be stranded on a desert island. Much like the radio programme, you are allowed to take certain things with you. However, these must be certain qualities you would like to find in the one other person who is going to be stranded with you. List the ten qualities you would most like that person to have. Remember you do not know how long you might have to spend with that person.

In smaller groups share your list. As a group come up with a joint list of the ten most important qualities.

Joining with others so that you now have two roughly equal groups, share their lists and now come up with the three most important qualities you would like to find in that person.

Coming back to one large group, share your decisions.

Now you must to come up with *one* quality which you all believe to be the most important of all; what would be the one quality you would most hope for?

### Questions for discussion

What do we understand by relational ministry?

Why is it important to us?

What is our strategic approach to its development in our church?

What are the basic skills needed to build relational ministry?

How do we develop positive, healthy, appropriate relationships with young people?

To what extent are we called to be

– friends?
– role models?

### Prayer

Listen to *Just walk with me* being read aloud.

# Just walk with me

*I have a problem.* I want to tell you about it. No, I really don't. I'd rather keep it to myself; handle it alone. I do think it would be good for me to share it with you, though. I don't want to because of what you'll say or how you'll act.

*I'm afraid* you might feel sorry for me in a way that makes me feel pathetic. Like I'm some 'poor thing'.

*I'm afraid* you'll try to cheer me up. That you will give me words, or texts or prayers that tell me in a subtle way to stop feeling bad. If you do that I'll feel worse (but hide it behind my obedient cheerful smile). I'll feel you don't understand. I'll feel you are making light of my problem (if it can be brushed away with some brief words of cheer).

*I'm afraid* you'll give me an answer. That this problem I've been wrestling with for some time now and about which I have thought endless thoughts will be belittled. You can answer in a half-minute what I've struggled with for weeks.

*I'm afraid* also you might ignore my problem; talk quickly about other things, tell me of your own.

*I'm afraid* too you might see me as stronger than I am. Not needing you to listen and care. (It's true, I can get along alone, but I shouldn't have to.)

What I'd really like is if you would 'just walk with me'. Listen, as I begin in some blundering, clumsy way to break through my fearfulness of being exposed as weak. Hold my hand and pull me gently as I falter and begin to draw back. Say a word, make a motion, or a sound that says, 'I'm with you.' If you've been where I am, tell me how you felt in a way that I can know you're trying to walk with me – not change me.

*But I'm afraid . . .*
> You'll think I'm too weak to deserve respect and responsibility . . .
> You'll explain what's happening to me with labels and interpretation . . .
> Or you'll ask me, 'What'ya going to do about it?'

PLEASE, *just walk with me.* All those other things seem so much brighter and sharper, smarter, and expert. But what really takes Love is 'Just Walk with Me'.

*I'm sure*, what I want is people who have a Shepherd as their model. People who in their own way bring to others an experience of:
*The Lord is my Shepherd, I shall not want . . . Yes even when I walk through the valley, You're with me . . . (walking with me).*

Source: Institute for Professional Youth Ministry

# 5 Using Groups

## Why?

In the last few chapters we have been exploring how to lay foundations for a holistic church youth ministry. Every church reading this book will be at a different stage with a completely different shape to their youth ministry. In this chapter we will look at the possibilities for different types of organized groups and meetings that could be offered by a church. This exploration is helpful to make in the early stages of a youth ministry because it enables broad

### This chapter will help you:

✔ identify some of the options;

✔ consider what would suit your church;

✔ prepare and plan for a youth-group meeting – setting goals, aims and objectives;

✔ think through resources available to you;

✔ evaluate your progress.

vision and opens up the possibilities for the church, but it shouldn't be a deterrent! This chapter is not prescriptive – you do not have to establish all, or any, of the different types of groups and meetings we will look at. But if you are looking to establish a regular meeting point for young people or build on to an existing youth group programme then you may want to think about developing some organized activity using the following thoughts in your preparation.

# The possibilities

Below are some of the options for groups and meetings. Use them to spark off ideas of your own, you will probably also be aware of other initiatives in neighbouring churches – plagiarize if they work for you too!

## Youth group

### What is it?

Although often used as a generic term, it is most commonly used to describe a regular meeting for a designated age group, most commonly with a predominantly social programme.

### Typical activities:

Almost anything and everything! Usually a mixed programme, which could include videos, talks, programmes delivered by visiting leaders/experts, games, themed evenings, issue-based discussions, sports, drama, music and food (snacks or one-off barbecues or meals). Later we will look at regular activity-related groups, but a youth group is the ideal place to have a one-off drama evening or tennis tournament in which everyone can have a go.

### Useful for:

New youth ministries where it is felt important to establish a regular meeting point for young people or perhaps as a social balance to a programme of more intense focus, say in a church which offers confirmation classes and a Bible study group. A youth group can make an ideal venue for welcoming young people not already connected with the church, either alongside more involved young people or as a new outreach initiative.

### Ideal age groups:

All ages can benefit from a youth group, but do read the later paragraph on defining boundaries (see page 48) to think through whether the group will have an age restriction.

### Suggested venues:

Determined according to size – the church hall is often ideal or a narthex (porch) or sanctuary of the church if available, but consider a more neutral venue if your youth group has been established to appeal to young people not yet connected with the church. Smaller groups may like to start in a home to encourage a feeling of intimacy. Almost any venue will work, though schools are often less successful with older young people.

## House group

### What is it?

A smaller group meeting in someone's home, perhaps one of a network of several house groups. The usual size is 6–8 plus group leaders.

### Typical activities:

House groups are typically discussion based, sometimes established to follow a short course or choosing to use a course for part of their programme. Examples of these could be a video or Lent course, or a Youth Alpha course. Groups that are part of a larger network can benefit from all following the same material, with responsibility for preparation shared between all the leaders, rather than the onus being on the individual group leaders.

### Useful for:

House groups can be a successful complement to a youth group in churches with a large group with a predominantly social programme. They offer members the opportunity for discussion in a more necessarily intimate grouping and to build close relationships with fellow house-group members. Groups could be according to age/gender/interest as needed to complement the make-up of the larger youth group.

### Ideal age groups:

House groups are most commonly offered to young people aged 13–14+, but there is no reason for them not to be offered to younger people. For groups whose discussions are issue-based, it can be useful to offer young people a group of members fairly close in age so that they can identify with common experiences. However, house groups also make an ideal place for inter-age discussion and learning, perhaps bringing young people and adults together to follow a Lent course. Care must be given in training the leaders of such groups to maximize the all-age potential.

## Suggested venues:

Houses are obviously the most ideal, offering comfortable furniture, smaller spaces and refreshments conducive to comfortable sharing and discussion. The meetings could be held in, or rotate around, the homes of church members who are willing to donate their living room, mugs of coffee and biscuits, this being a good way of involving the church in supporting the ministry, without asking the owners to lead a group. Similarly the meetings could rotate around the homes of group members, but you should check with parents first and be sensitive to group members who would find hosting the group in their home difficult because of personal or financial circumstances.

## Confirmation group

### What is it?

A confirmation group is normally a designated age group pulled together to prepare for confirmation. Traditionally these have been run by a member of clergy, but this need not always be so. Successful confirmation preparation has been offered by full-time youth workers and lay leaders – perhaps in a team with a member of clergy involved and session leading equally shared amongst the leadership team. Some groups who have been through confirmation preparation together remain together as an ongoing house or study group, some churches offer an open post-confirmation group.

## Typical activities:

Many churches have their own developed course, particularly common where members of clergy take responsibility for confirmation preparation. Others follow ready-to-use material, often developing a mix from two or three resources.

Post-confirmation groups can be similar to house groups and might use prepared courses or resources.

## Useful for:

Obviously in confirmation preparation! Post-confirmation groups can offer ongoing spiritual support and exploration for young Christians, this being a common age-group at which young people drop out of church community.

## Ideal age groups:

This will be dependent on denominational ruling for confirmation. Confirmation groups can be run extremely successfully as inter-age groups, provided due care is given to the preparation and delivery of the sessions. In confirmation perhaps more than anywhere else, new Christians can be at their most vulnerable.

## Suitable venues:

As with house groups, though larger groups will obviously need an appropriate size of venue. You may want to consider dividing a larger group into smaller groups to encourage an intimacy and security for participants.

## Prayer group

### What is it?

A prayer group meets to offer prayer for issues where it perceives prayer is needed – either at the request of others or the determination of group members. Many youth ministries find that Bible study and a prayer meeting sit companionably in one group – often as equal halves of a meeting.

## Typical activities:

Prayer groups commonly offer a time of guided prayer followed by open prayer. Many prayer groups have a facility for church members to make prayer requests – perhaps through a prayer book kept in the church for example. Again, guided prayer material is available, though more commonly written with adult groups in mind.

## Useful for:

Obviously the benefits of prayer go unsaid. A dedicated prayer group can offer the chance for its members to contribute to the church and can give members resources for personal structured prayer time. A prayer group can also be established occasionally, for example for a particular church project or festival, e.g. during Holy Week.

## Ideal age groups:

Again, suitable for all ages and a great inter-age activity. Be sure to give clear guidance to members as to how the structure works – open prayer time can be extremely daunting and even embarrassing for those who don't know what is expected and appropriate. Ensure that meeting lengths are age appropriate.

## Suitable venues:

As with house groups, though, larger groups will obviously need an appropriate size of venue. You may want to consider dividing a larger group into smaller groups to encourage an intimacy and security for participants.

## Bible study group

### What is it?

A Bible study group meet to read and discuss Bible passages, usually in a sequential order, or following a prepared course.

### Typical activities:

Bible study groups often follow a thematic approach to the Bible or a particular book, e.g.

writings about forgiveness, the letters of St Paul. Many groups follow a prepared course of session outlines and share the leadership around the group, but there is no reason why an experienced leader can't prepare their own material.

## Ideal age groups:

As with prayer groups, suitable for all ages and inter-age groups.

## Suitable venues:

As with house groups, though larger groups will obviously need an appropriate size of venue. You may want to consider dividing a larger group into smaller groups to encourage an intimacy and security for participants.

## Breakfast club

### What is it?

A breakfast club, as it name suggests, is a group that meets for breakfast and is usually the same concept as a house group – meeting for discussion or to follow a course or programme, perhaps a time for Bible study.

### Typical activities:

Breakfast (which can be as simple as toast and coffee) with discussion, either over breakfast or immediately afterwards.

### Useful for:

The idea is to offer those attending an alternative time for a group meeting other than an evening. This is great for churches whose young people are already involved in several after-school and evening activities, but be sure to consult young people as to when they will realistically appear for breakfast. A breakfast club also offers another opportunity for church members to get involved by preparing the breakfast.

### Ideal age groups:

Suitable for all ages and inter-age groups.

## Suitable venues:

Groups could meet in homes or gather in a larger hall for breakfast and then group in small areas around the church and hall buildings as available to you.

## Drama group

### What is it?

A drama group would normally meet for a specific programme of drama, whether to prepare for a one-off production or as an ongoing group. A church might include a drama workshop as part of a church weekend or away-day of mission which might lead to the establishing of a drama group.

### Typical activities:

A drama group might have the specific brief of preparing drama for use in worship once a month, say, or may simply wish to use drama and have fun without the pressure of preparing a performance. Such a drama group would normally engage in a variety of drama games and exercises, perhaps coupled with trips to the theatre, critiquing a video and visits from a local 'expert' in stage make-up or circus skills for example. A group meeting to rehearse a performance would probably wish to start with games and exercises to warm up, followed by the rehearsal. Drama groups traditionally tend to be run by those with some drama experience, but there are resources to help those with little or no experience to offer a balanced programme with occasional help from visiting leaders from local amateur groups and professional theatre companies.

### Useful for:

Offering young people a chance to contribute to church worship by either occasionally or regularly preparing a piece of drama for the Sunday or special services. Drama is great for communication, confidence building and group cohesion skills and is a way of bringing young people into contact with the church in a fun way. Drama can be a particularly successful 'leveller' in churches with a diverse socio-economic and/or ability make-up. Across-church productions, such as Christmas pantomimes, are an excellent opportunity for inter-age activity.

### Suitable venues:

Ideally a hall or part of the church with sufficient space to move around and where the group are not overlooked and do not disturb others when being noisy.

## Sports/activity group

### What is it?

A group which meets to enjoy a particular sport or activity.

### Typical activities:

Anything from football to computer games. Usually the meeting time will focus on the activity of the group, perhaps followed by a time of discussion or prayer.

### Useful for:

Reaching young people through their interests, building on the concept of holistic ministry and building strong relationships between leaders and members.

### Ideal age groups:

Any age group can enjoy such a group, but obvious consideration should be given to ensuring the safety of all members and leaders.

### Suitable venues:

This will obviously depend on the activity in question. Be sure to publicize the meeting venue to all to whom the group is open. Even though a basketball club might attract the same young people almost every week, it is important that the young person who has plucked up the courage to attend for the first time knows where and when to turn up.

## Holiday club/playscheme

### What is it?

Normally a day, afternoon or week of activities on a theme held at festivals and/or in school holidays.

### Typical activities:

Usually centred around a theme or a particular festival, they tend to be activity-based, with a mixed programme of, perhaps, music, arts and crafts, drama, worship, games, sports, outings or local trips. There are several resources available from one-off activity ideas to a full week's worth of hour-by-hour plans.

### Useful for:

Providing regular youth activity when term-time or weeknight activities are difficult for a church. Involving several members of the congregation in many ways from preparing refreshments to helping with the arts and crafts. Congregation members can easily contribute their expertise, for example a playscheme taking 'creation' as its theme could include a visit to a local farmer's land and animals. Holiday clubs and playschemes are a great outreach opportunity, parents with young children are nearly always keen to involve their children in activities throughout the school holidays, a meeting point for parents can also be provided alongside the holiday club.

### Ideal age groups:

Particularly, but not exclusively, suitable for children of primary school age. Teenagers often enjoy contributing to the ministry by helping in the leadership team and in the planning of the activities.

### Suitable venues:

Anywhere large enough! You will determine the maximum number of children you can accommodate according to the number of leaders and the size of venue you have available. You will probably want space for children to get outside at some point during the day/week, and more than one room in case you wish to divide the group for activities. The church can make an ideal venue, provided noise and mess from activities aren't going to be a problem.

## Good practice and Health and Safety

In Chapter 3 we looked at good practice in youth work when recruiting and training youth leaders. When establishing any meeting for young people, whether as a one-off or regular group, we must be equally mindful of good practice in our youth leaders and in our choice and use of venues. To be sure of best possible practice in terms of Health and Safety implications, consult your denominational youth officer for advice and support. This area can seem daunting and off-putting on your own. They will have experience in this area and be ready and equipped to help you.

There are certain legal restrictions on the length of meeting times and venue facilities for some age groups, particularly for under 8s. In certain situations you may be required to register with Social Services. The requirements of the law are not in themselves difficult to follow and should not make an activity prohibitive, they are obviously there to offer maximum protection to the children we serve and to ourselves. Social Services are keen to support and offer help to the voluntary sector regardless of whether you are required to register. The simplest route to finding all the information you need to comply with the law is to talk to your denominational children's or youth officer, who can guide you through the law as it pertains to your particular situation. If you do not have access to such a person, then contact your local Social Services Under Eights Officer.

Ensure that consideration is given to the emotional safety of young people by making sure that the venue you choose is conducive to the activity, i.e. comfortable, more intimate spaces for small group discussion, large soundproof spaces for large group games or sports, etc. Always ensure access to facilities for plenty of refreshments.

# Defining boundaries

## Age groups:

We have looked at ideal age groups in the above examples of meetings and groups, but each church will be different. In a rural church, offering two groups one for, say, 12–14-year-olds and another for 14+ year-olds is unlikely to be feasible. However, it is important to consider young people's needs within the aims and objectives of the group. Consider whether a 12-year-old and a 16-year-old are likely to get the maximum benefit from being in the same housegroup when discussing life choices such as relationships or career options.

If you have small numbers and/or they span a wide age range, why not offer a split meeting at the same time and in the same venue, splitting into age groups as appropriate for all or part of the meeting? Don't feel pressured to provide for every possible age group either. Why not start a Sunday morning breakfast club for 10–12-year-olds as they begin to leave Sunday School, then offer an evening youth group for those aged 12+ as the group grows older and begins to outgrow the breakfast club? Ask the young people for their opinions and help. You could also consider grouping by school year rather than age.

Whatever you decide is appropriate for your church, it is important to stick with your decision. If your lower age limit is 12, it isn't fair to allow one 11½-year-old to be part of the group. It can be difficult for the older members of the group if the dynamics become younger, for the other 11½-year-old not allowed to join the group, for those members who waited patiently until they were 12 to join the group and for the new member who is younger than the rest of the group.

## Rules and regulations:

Every group, however informal and of whatever age, survives by developing rules and regulations

whether or not they articulate them. You will want your group to be aware of the Health and Safety issues discussed, i.e. fire-drill procedure, physical boundaries of the meeting area (e.g. no access to the hall stage, stay within the lines of the football field) and these need to be clearly stated to the group as early as possible so that there is no room for misunderstanding or accidents. Many groups find it helpful to share these with the assembled group and then send the young people away with a copy of these rules, or to display them in the meeting area. You will need to decide what is best for your particular group.

In terms of behaviour rules, why not turn this over to the group for group consensus – taking time in a group meeting to discuss and determine what is and isn't acceptable behaviour by group members in meeting times? Groups who develop their own code of conduct are far more likely to own it and thus stick to it. Why not allocate time in an early meeting for the group to develop this contract? Ask members to list the things they wish to be included and decide what should happen in the event of the contract being broken by a member. It is best to do this after the group has met, so that the members have a clearer understanding of the dynamics and areas for potential difficulties that should be included. Again, consider printing these to display in the meeting area or to give to young people. Remember that all new members of the groups should be given a copy of these rules too.

# What would suit your church?

Before any new groups or meetings are introduced to your church's ministry, ensure that you take time to discuss the proposal with your church council (or body which has taken responsibility for oversight of the youth ministry), the volunteer team and the young people.

Ask yourselves the following questions:

- What groups are we currently enjoying?
- What do our young people want – what would they attend?

- What would complement what we are currently doing for our young people?

- What can we realistically manage in terms of time, venue, frequency, available leadership and cost?

- Who is going to be responsible for overseeing the new initiative?

- What resources are available to help us?

- When and how will we evaluate the new initiative?

Remember regular doesn't have to mean weekly! It is far better to offer something fortnightly or monthly and keep the leaders, members and activities fresh and positive. You can always increase the frequency as you grow and as resources permit.

# Getting ready and getting going

Once you have decided to deliver a new type of group or meeting in your youth ministry, it is imperative that sufficient time is allowed for adequate preparation. Although it is tempting to jump straight into a new group and sort out the details as you go along, there is rarely time to put details into place once a group is up and running and developing. Adequate preparation ensures that all who approach the group feel as fully prepared and on top of the practical details as possible. The more preparation is done, the more time leaders will have available to focus on building relationships with the young people. Taking time to think through why you are doing what you are doing aids the confidence of new (and even aspiring) volunteers and ensures a focused meeting for participants.

When preparing for a meeting, there are three key questions to think through. These are:

What are our **goals** for the group?

What are our **aims** for the group?

What are our **objectives** for the group?

These are familiar terms to many people, for which I would like to suggest the following definitions:

**Goals:** What are our long-term dreams for the group? How do these tie in with our youth ministry's mission statement?

**Aims:** What are we going to do to achieve our goals?

**Objectives:** What are *all* the practical steps we need to take to achieve our aims?

Objectives should be **SMART**:

>  **Specific**;
>
>  **Measurable**;
>
>  **Achievable**;
>
>  **Realistic**;
>
>  **Timed**.

Apply this to each objective and see if you are being SMART.

Let us take as an example St Swithin's church. St Swithin's has previously had a large Sunday School for those aged 5–11. A serious look at its youth ministry has resulted in the decision to start a social youth group for 11–14-year-olds. Its goal is to meet the needs of those growing out of Sunday School and to begin to connect with other young people in the area who have no connection with the church. St Swithin's has formed a planning team and a volunteer team to support them in their development of this trial term. The planning team is directly answerable to the church council. The planning team comprises four adults and two young people, one from the Sunday School and one who is not currently involved in the church community. St Swithin's youth group planning team might answer these questions as follows:

# First meeting of the planning team for St Swithin's youth group

## Goals

We dream of a youth group that is accessible to young people in the area who currently have no connection with the church, but that is also appropriate for the young people currently involved in our church life.

## Aims

Based on our research across the church, we are going to establish a fortnightly youth group on Sunday nights. We will start by offering a trial term (Autumn term) and will offer a programme of social activities. At the end of the term we will evaluate the success of the group and decide whether or not to continue.

## Objectives

In order to prepare properly we need to do the following things:

| ACTION | Who? | When? | Done? |
|---|---|---|---|
| Ensure hall is available and book | Jane | a.s.a.p. | |
| Draw up programme of activities | planning team | by 15th July | |
| Invite specialist leaders | Marion | by end of July | |
| Report back to church council, article in newsletter and parish magazine | Sarah Dave | over summer, increase in September | |
| Prepare and distribute posters – church noticeboard, local schools, local burger bar, football club | Jane | end of August | |
| Prepare future meetings for planning team, including one on-site to run through Health and Safety | planning team | ongoing | |
| Arrange future training session for leaders | Dave to contact | by early September | |
| Buy refreshments | Jane | by first meeting | |

The questions of goals, aims, and objectives are the fundamental questions to be asked at every preparation meeting, so once our planning team have moved on and are, say, planning the third meeting of their trial term, their goals, aims and objectives might be as follows:

# Sixth meeting of the planning team for St Swithin's youth group
## Planning for youth group meeting three

### Goals

This term our goals are to establish a regular group that enjoys meeting together for a variety of social activities in which everyone is able to take part, no-one feels left out and all who want to feel that they can come along.

### Aims

Each week we will offer a different activity. In week three we will have an American theme night, in which those present will be invited to try some American youth group activities and food and think about fellow young Christians in America. Because some people will be coming for the first time, we have decided not to ask people to dress up on this occasion.

### Objectives

Our activities for the evening will be:

Soft baseball;

Making popcorn;

Establishing penpal links with our link church in Oregon;

Watching *The Simpsons* video – followed by small discussion on issues raised;

Prayers from America;

American camp fire songs;

To prepare for this we need to:

| ACTION | Who? | When? | Done? |
|---|---|---|---|
| Prepare and distribute Stars and Stripes poster | Jane | by 2nd meeting | |
| Follow up church's link with Oregon, set up penpal link | Sarah | by middle of September | |
| Talk to Camp America office in London to find prayers and camp fire songs | Marion | by meeting | |
| Choose and video episode of 'The Simpsons' and prepare group leaders with discussion questions | Dave | by next planning meeting | |
| Check refreshment stock | Jane | ongoing | |
| Organize equipment and materials | Sarah | by the meeting | |
| Set up meeting area | Dave Marion | on the day | |

# Resources

There are many resources on the market which can provide you with a full term's meeting plans or a one-off activity. The choice can be overwhelming and obviously not all the resources (and these are mostly in book or video format) are going to be relevant for your group. Most leaders find trying a few different resources necessary and many will use a pick-and-mix approach to create meeting plans for their particular group.

If you're lucky enough to have a Christian resources library or lending facility in your area take full advantage. If not, a morning spent with a chair, notebook and pen in your local Christian bookshop may be an effective alternative. Again, spend time with your denominational youth officer or resources centre staff, who should be aware of the broad cross-section of resources available and help you to elicit the resources most likely to be relevant to your group. Do seek help when setting out – resources should be helpful and equipping for the leaders, not so daunting as to leave you floundering.

# Evaluation

Evaluation is important to the survival of any group and its leaders, ensuring that it is still meeting the needs of its members and fulfilling its aims and objectives. If you find that it is no longer doing this, it is not necessarily a bad thing – maybe the aims and objectives need revising to accommodate the group's development.

Use the sample questionnaire in this chapter, *How are we doing?*, as an **evaluation tool**, and share it with the planning team, leaders, members and parents too. Once collated and discussed by those with the responsibility for planning and delivering the group, share the findings with those who contributed to the evaluation, perhaps through a special meeting or newsletter.

# How are we doing?

Name of group:.................................................................................

Please take time to answer the following questions about our group; we want to hear *your* views!

All evaluations will be read by ...................................................... and then discussed by........................................

We will report back to you on........................

What do you most enjoy about the group and why?

What do you least enjoy and why?

What would you like to see the group do more of?

The aims of our group are  .......................................................................
.................................................................................

How well do you think we are fulfilling these aims?

Any other comments?

I am (please tick as appropriate)

❑    A group member

❑    A leader

❑    A parent

Thank you for your time!

## Summary

### The questions to ask:

- What groups are we currently enjoying in our church?

- What do we need in order to complement our existing programme and meet the needs of our young people?

- How do good practice guidelines impact and support our plans?

- What are our goals, aims and objectives for each new initiative?

- What resources are available?

### Points for action:

- hold fourth meeting using the following **session outline**;

- consider your church's needs and plan accordingly;

- activate a team responsible for planning, delivery and evaluation;

- seek advice and support in ensuring you comply with Health and Safety guidelines;

- develop a Health and Safety checklist for your church when engaged in youth ministry activity.

### Useful resources:

- John Buckeridge (ed.), *Youthwork Magazine*, Christian Communications Partnership

- Denominational Youth Officer and Resource Centre

- M. Kindred, *Once Upon A Group*, Michael Kindred, 1987

- Local Authority Youth Service

- *On The Way: Towards an Integrated Approach to Christian Initiation,* Church House Publishing, 1998

- Denny Rydberg, *Building Community in Youth Groups*, Group Books, Colorado, 1985

## Exploring youth ministry 4

### Session 4 outline

#### Resources needed:
- flipchart and pens, list of different groups already written;
- a copy of the *Young person's profile sheet* (page 58) for each person;
- young people's completed questionnaires (page 53) or tape of recorded discussion (if needed);
- **group notes** copied as a handout for each person – these could be distributed prior to the meeting;
- **facilitator's notes** for the discussion facilitator;
- a copy of the questionaire used as an **evaluation tool** for each person.

#### Prayer (5 minutes)
Gather the group together in silence and say, 'Lord God, we ask you to be with us as we approach this discussion. We ask for your gifts of creativity and discernment. Help us to approach this discussion with an open mind, from an objective viewpoint and with a willingness to learn. Amen.'

#### Opening activity (10 minutes)
Divide the group into three small groups and give each group one of the 'profiles' from the following *Young person's profile sheet*. Ask the group to respond to their outlined young person by developing a menu of youth ministry activities that would offer a holistic approach to the young person detailed. Gather the group together and allow each small group to feed back.

#### Discussion (60 minutes)
Ask someone in the group to act as 'scribe' if you feel it is appropriate.

The facilitator should lead the group through the discussion questions. A suggested timing is given which can be adapted to suit your church's needs.

#### Summarizing and moving on (10 minutes)
Go through the discussion notes with the large group. Assign any action to be taken to members of the group and detail the deadline for completing the action. Ask for group consensus on the action list and note who will be responsible for distributing the lists and by when. Confirm arrangements for the next session.

#### Prayer (5 minutes)
Gather together and say, 'Lord, we come to you and offer our discussion and action list for your blessing. We have begun to explore how youth ministry should be like a cafeteria, offering different items on the menu to appeal to each of us. Now we would like to thank you for some of the different items on our church's menu. [Invite members to give thanks for individual activities of the church.] We thank you and are proud to call you our heavenly Father. Amen.'

### Facilitator's notes

#### What groups are we currently enjoying? (5 minutes)
List specific groups currently running. Don't worry if yours is a new youth ministry and you don't as yet have any activities running.

## What do our young people want? What would they attend? (15 minutes)

This will involve hearing from young people. If you have used the **evaluation tool** on page 53, you can bring the questionnaire responses to this meeting; if not, use the questions as a basis for discussion with young people. If you do not have any young people attending the session, you will need to involve some – this is not a question for speculative answers from adults, or the implemented groups are likely to miss the mark. If you feel it would be inappropriate to 'wheel in' young people for this session, why not ask another member of the volunteer team to tape a discussion with some of the young people with whom they work, and play the tape at this point. Again, the questionnaire can form the basis for the discussion. If your youth ministry is not yet active, why not bring young people in your church community or in families of your church community together to meet with you to make a recording.

## What would complement what we are currently doing for young people? (15 minutes)

Draw people to the different types of groups listed in this chapter, list them on the flipchart and encourage the group to add to the list of options.

Then think through which, if any, of the different groups might complement your current youth ministry.

## What can we realistically manage in terms of time, venue, frequency, available leadership and cost? (10 minutes)

Be specific and realistic, remember that one small step done well is far more effective than trying to offer too much too thinly spread.

## Who is going to be responsible for overseeing the new initiative? (5 minutes)

Again, be specific and realistic, detail who is to take responsibility for both the planning and delivery of each new initiative. Whilst the planning team and delivery team have to overlap, consider whether it would split the workload to divide it between two teams.

## What resources are available to help us? (5 minutes)

It may be appropriate here to appoint some researchers, or to involve your denominational youth officer.

## When and how will we evaluate the new initiative? (5 minutes)

As we have discussed, this is imperative to the ongoing success of any initiative and will prevent it existing in isolation from the rest of the ministry. Agree on the frequency of evaluations and put dates into diaries before you finish.

## Exploring youth ministry 4

### Prayer

'Lord God, we ask you to be with us as we approach this discussion. We ask for your gifts of creativity and discernment. Help us to approach this discussion with an open mind, from an objective viewpoint and with a willingness to learn. Amen.'

## Opening activity

In three small groups you will be given one of the 'profiles' from the following *Young person's profile sheet*. Respond to the outlined young person by developing a menu of youth ministry activities that would offer a holistic approach to the young person detailed.

As a large group share your suggested 'menus'.

## Questions for discussion

What groups are we currently enjoying?

What do our young people want? What would they attend?

What would complement what we are currently doing for young people?

What can we realistically manage in terms of time, venue, frequency, available leadership and cost?

Who is going to be responsible for overseeing the new initiative?

What resources are available to help us?

When and how will we evaluate the new initiative?

### Prayer

'Lord, we come to you and offer our discussion and action list for your blessing. We have begun to explore how youth ministry should be like a cafeteria, offering different items on the menu to appeal to each of us. Now we would like to thank you for some of the different items on our church's menu. [Group members now give thanks for individual activities of the church]. We thank you and are proud to call you our heavenly Father. Amen.'

Photocopiable

# Young person's profile sheet

## 1. Amy

Amy is 13. She lives in the new housing development on the edge of her rural parish. She did attend the local Church school, but now she is at secondary school she hasn't been into the church for two years. Her family are not church members, but would support her involvement. Amy knows a couple of girls in her class at school who go to the Sunday morning club, but she doesn't feel she knows them well enough to go along with them, although it does sound like fun and Amy did enjoy being part of the church when she attended at primary school.

What could the church offer that would appeal to Amy's needs?

## 2. Sam

Sam is 17. She is taking her A Levels at college and has been part of the church for as long as she can remember. She has been confirmed and, until she started at college, attended the Sunday night youth group. However, she now feels too old for that and is beginning to feel a little isolated at church. There is only one other guy who is the same age but she doesn't really know him. Sam is getting despondent and has begun to stop coming to Sunday services.

What could the church offer to meet Sam's needs?

## 3. John

John is 15 and has never been near the church. He sees some of his classmates going into the church hall for some kind of youth group on a Wednesday and, although he secretly thinks it might be fun, John would never go along. He's afraid of looking stupid if he doesn't know what it's all about. He also thinks people might laugh at him if they knew he was interested.

What could the church offer to meet John's needs?

# 6 Responding to Families

## Who?

Everyone is a member of a family. Regardless of its size, structure or patterns of communication and contact, we are all members of a family, although each of us has a slightly different understanding of what we mean by the word. For a young person, the awareness of, and relationship to, their family is perhaps more heightened than for an adult. For the young person who is not yet living independently, their experience of domestic and relational structures is current and is limited to that of theirfamily set-up – be it in a home with two parents, a single parent, a foster home or with extended family.

### This chapter will help you:

✔ explore how a youth ministry can embrace a young person's family situation;

✔ explore how to keep families informed, involved and supported.

Because most young people are still living within their family structure we must ensure we embrace this component of their lives fully to offer the holistic ministry we have already established as important. Of course we acknowledge that some young people choose to leave their family structure and live an independent life, but perhaps a fair summary of young people's living situations is to say that these are as a result of their family relationship whether this is positive or negative. Thus we must approach young people within their family background and living situation. (For ease of reference we will use the term family to summarize what we know to be different in the case of each young person, and the term parents to embrace the adult or adults having responsibility for the care of the young person.)

# How?

Offering a holistic ministry to embrace the family means ensuring that a youth ministry responds to the family structures of its young people and supports and complements the family. A youth ministry that tries to take young people out of their family situation and 'fix' them is offering the wrong relationship for young people. Youth ministry needs to work alongside the family, to embrace the family in its team approach. At its simplest level this can mean running activities at appropriate times during the evening or not offering a residential weekend for 16-year-olds during GCSE examination time. At a more complex level, this can mean involving parents in a disciplinary issue or supporting a young person in sharing personal information or a concern with their parents.

It is easy to see how we can practically complement the family structure of the young person, alongside offering appropriate meeting times for activities, i.e. not running late night meetings on school nights or during popular family mealtimes. Information and involvement are paramount to the success of the youth ministry.

# Informing families

First let us look at **information**; most of us will be familiar with informative notes outlining off-site activities run by the school and seeking parental consent. Such information is also important in any activity-based youth ministry, but I would advocate a broader approach of getting parents 'fully on board' with the youth ministry's mission. Already we have looked at informing the church and getting them involved with the new ministry. The same weight should also be given to informing and sharing with parents who may or may not be members of the congregation.

Consider holding an introductory meeting for the parents of young people, sharing the church's discussions and determined needs for a youth ministry and exploring the mission statement of the youth ministry – offer those present a chance to ask questions and feel comfortable with what you are offering their young people. Individual invitations work well for these kinds of meetings if you know your 'client group' of young people, outlining the purpose and agenda for the meeting so people know what they are coming to. Remember that families not connected to the church may well feel a little nervous about attending. Offer refreshments and a chance for people to meet one another.

Ongoing information is equally important and helps ensure that families know exactly what the young person isinvolved in. This can be particularly true with a new youth ministry where new things are being tried or progress may seem to be slow. Adults responsible for young people like to know where their young people are and what the purpose of the meeting/activity is. This is not to say that young people shouldn't have their own space and personal activity, but for the parent the knowledge that their charge is in a particular place at a particular time enjoying, say, a Bible study with adults who have the young person's best interests at heart, is extremely reassuring. Again, remember that if your particular church is engaged in dedicated outreach activity or offering, say, a youth group for young people not previously connected with the church, it is natural that there may be some concern or even suspicion from their families. Informing families fully of your intentions empowers them to help the young person make choices about their involvement. Why not consider a regular parents' newsletter with forthcoming significant dates, details of any volunteer team training, new ideas or PCC discussions? Involve young people in its preparation and offer information as is appropriate to the age of the young people with whom you work, e.g. a youth group for 7–10-year-olds will need to advise the family of exact meeting times to enable them to co-ordinate the young people's transportation, and indicate whether it is appropriate for them to come into the meeting area to collect the young people. Be careful with terminology here, though, as the use of *parent* may automatically exclude adults who are responsible for your young people but are not their birth parents. Consult with those attending an introductory meeting and come up with a suitable title and frequency of such a newsletter.

Obviously you will want parental consent for activities off-site or outside any usual meeting. Current good practice would also advise you to seek parental consent for the attendance of a minor at any youth group, confirmation class or other organized activity. Sample consent forms are included in Appendix 2. It would also be wise to advise parents of the good practice and child protection policies, including that the appropriate screening of all volunteers has taken place, as discussed with an appropriate professional (see Chapter 3).

## Involving families

Asking parents to arrange a transport rota is one way of involving them in supporting the youth ministry without getting involved in group leadership. This can overcome one of the dilemmas in youth ministry in that young people need time out of their family situation and a youth ministry can, and should, be their space. However, to survive, a youth ministry needs a certain number of members on its volunteer team and one of the most able and willing groups of people can often be the parents who see the value of the ministry and want to support and encourage it. You will need to consult with the parents and seek their support in resolving the dilemma. One solution is to ask parents to get involved with an alternative activity to the one in which their young person is involved, or to offer practical support rather than up-front leadership.

Another option is to form a pool of parents to rotate their involvement as leaders so that they are not involved in every meeting, avoiding over-

burdening them and giving the young people their own space. Remember that if you are asking parents to be involved in the volunteer team, they are subject to all the principles of good practice we looked at in Chapter 3, which means offering them the same recruitment, screening, training and maintenance that is offered to the rest of the volunteer team.

Involving parents must also mean more than requesting their help. Parents should also be involved in the decision-making process, involve them as visionaries at the outset, in ongoing monitoring and evaluation of the ministry. As well as ensuring that they are informed of decisions taken in the youth ministry, include them in the process of shaping the ministry and in ongoing decisions. Why not use this chapter's **session outline** as a meeting plan for an initial meeting with parents.

## Supporting families

A youth ministry can, and I would venture to suggest should, support parents. This can mean emotionally and practically. One church, St Michael and All Angels, responded to both of these needs by forming a two-way support group for parents, which took the first half of each group meeting to look at how parents could support the youth ministry and the second half to support the parents. In the first half of the meeting, the volunteer team shared with the parents the forthcoming plans and decisions to be made. The parents were able to offer practical and emotional support where needed. After coffee, parents had the chance to talk around issues of parenting, sometimes in small group discussion, sometimes as a large group with an invited speaker or informational video. The group was supportive in allowing parents the chance to talk, but never dictatorial. Interestingly, several members of the group went on to become committed members of the church.

All youth ministries can support parents by the perspective from which they approach young people. Let us look a little more closely at an example:

*Dorothy, a full-time youth minister in a group of rural churches in Suffolk, and Andy, a volunteer, ran a weekly discussion and Bible study group for their young people aged 14+. The group decided that it would like to look at the issue of parenting in a forthcoming meeting. Dorothy and Andy were delighted that the initiative had come from the young people and came to the meeting prepared to let the young people speak about whatever was on their minds. They saw the purpose of the meeting as exploring issues around parenting, hopefully being able to encourage young people to see issues of conflict from their parents' perspective and perhaps even moving into issues of teenage pregnancy and parenting. Dorothy and Andy were prepared for an open and frank discussion and planned the meeting accordingly. After some initial social time, Andy opened with an activity asking the young people to describe their parents anonymously on a piece of paper which would then be put into a hat. When the first person came to pick an anonymous description to read, the group howled with laughter at the derogatory statements made about a member's dad and were quick to attribute various fathers to the description, which caused even more hilarity. Dorothy and Andy were surprised at how the activity had gone, thinking that the descriptions would be of the parents' physical appearance. Almost all of the descriptions were the same and the group's amusement and fun with the activity was contagious. Andy and Dorothy found themselves laughing and joining in with the jokes. The evening continued in the same vein and, although the young people were able to get some of their frustrations with their parents 'off their chests', there had not been the opportunity to draw something constructive from the meeting or to address any of the issues that Dorothy and Andy had hoped would be addressed. Dorothy and Andy had, inadvertently, been completely unsupportive of the young people's families by being seen to condone the condemning of them in*

*the meeting. Sadly, the ramifications of this went beyond an inadvertent derision of the group's parents. Some of the young people took the meeting's discussion home and shared it with their parents who were, understandably, very hurt and upset. Not only were they then more sceptical about the particular group, but also became less trusting of the youth ministry as a whole. This made it difficult for Dorothy and Andy and also for the young people, who found themselves caught in a conflict situation, wanting to have their freedom and space within the group but not wanting to cause distress to their parents.*

So what could they have done to offer a meeting that was supportive both to the parents and to the young people? Clearly it would have been inappropriate to have clamped down on all fun or not to have allowed the young people to express some of their frustrations. In being too authoritarian in their approach to the activity and the subsequent meeting, they would have run the risk of being unsupportive of the young people's needs and frustrations. To have offered a balanced meeting that supported the young people from their families' perspective, Dorothy and Andy could have:

1.  clarified further the purpose of the discussion with the young people so that they could have been better prepared;

2.  been aware of the possible misinterpretation of the opening activity and been clear about their expectations in the instructions;

3.  set some ground rules as a group at the beginning of the meeting, outlining that negative comments would be acceptable provided they were substantiated rather than unjustified moaning;

4.  invited some parents to contribute – either at the meeting, possibly inviting parents of teenagers not involved in the group – or beforehand through research – perhaps a questionnaire which could have been shared with the young people;

5. offered some follow-up to the meeting, perhaps even inviting parents to this meeting to explore some of the issues raised.

Young people come to the youth ministry from their family situation, whatever structure that may have. They are shaped by their family experience and history and, when they leave contact with any youth ministry activity, they return to their family situation. If a youth ministry chooses not to acknowledge this, they choose not to acknowledge one of the most fundamental and influential aspects of a young person's life. Regardless of our personal opinion of a young person's family situation, we must offer a ministry that reaches the whole young person. To deny where the young person has come from is to deny ministering to part of that young person. This means offering a ministry that is appropriate, embracing and supportive of the young person within their family.

The following resources may be helpful when considering direct ministry to families: the outline for a parent/child *Talking shop* and the *Two-way support meeting* outline. The *Two-way support meeting* is a useful tool for either a one-off or regular meeting of parents and the youth ministry volunteer team to offer support to one another. The parent/child *Talking shop* is ideally conducted around a meal which allows the parents and their child/children the opportunity to answer the questions. As the outline suggests, perhaps the wardens or church staff could cook the meal for the group. The *Talking shop* works particularly well with a large group; the activities questions could be adapted onto cards for families to use at home if a large group gathering is not possible.

# Meeting outline: Two-way support group for parents, guardians and adults responsible for young people

## Resources:
- Bible with passages marked (if to be used);
- flipchart with small-group questions (if to be used).

## Prayer (5 minutes)
You will need to consider whether this group is used to praying in meetings, if so, use the opening and closing prayers in the **session outline.**

## Opening activity (10 minutes)
Ask those gathered to pair up with someone they do not know. Ask them to find out from their partner the answers to the following questions:

What is your name?

What is your favourite flavour of ice cream?

What is your least favourite television programme?

What is one activity your family likes to do together?

Ask each pair to link up with another pair and introduce one another.

## Supporting parents (30 minutes)
You might like to invite a speaker to address the group or to watch an educational video together. Or you might like to use the following format in small groups. This format can be used regularly; small groups may like to meet as a group at subsequent meetings. You may like to copy these questions onto a flipchart for all to see:

Tell us about your young person, describe him/her.

What has been one recent highlight in your relationship with your young person?

What has been one concern for you as an adult responsible for this young person?

## Refreshment break (10 minutes)

## Supporting the youth ministry
(20 minutes)

This is your chance to share new ideas, policies or concerns for discussion and seek help as appropriate. If you are seeking practical support or action, make sure you attribute responsibility to the appropriate people. Record the action list and ensure that it is distributed promptly.

## Details of next meeting (10 minutes)

Use this time to confirm arrangements for the next meeting, take suggestions for discussion topics or visiting speakers for future meetings.

## Prayer (5 minutes)

If appropriate, use the closing prayer from this chapter's **session outline** on page 72.

# Meeting outline: Parent and child talking shop

It is suggested that the following meeting is conducted around a meal. If the logistics of this prove too difficult, ensure that suitable refreshments are available. For ease of reference here, we have used the terms 'parent' and 'child'; ensure you use appropriate terminology for your group.

## Resources:

- large sheets of paper and pens;

- dice for *Treasured moments* (page 65);

- copies of the *Food* questions (page 66) for each course copied onto cards for each family group (you could make double-sided copies that can stand in the middle of the table and be easily seen by everyone in the pair/family group);

- statement cards for *Affirmation* (page 67);

- night-light candle for each person (page 67);

- meal or refreshments.

# Treasured moments

If you are a large gathering then it would be best to subdivide into smaller groups for this activity. Groups should be of about a dozen in size, with a mixture of ages. The group should then sit in a circle and members then take it in turns to talk about the place that they most treasure and why.

After everyone has been given a chance to share their most treasured place, look at the list below. You might like to put just one large copy of the list somewhere in the middle of the group for everyone to see. Each member then takes his/her turn to throw a dice and talk on the subject that corresponds to the number thrown.

1.  The holiday you most treasure

2.  The birthday you most treasure

3.  The Christmas you most treasure

4.  A treasured moment with a parent or relative

5.  A treasured childhood moment

6.  A meal or certain food that has treasured memories

Allow time for all members of the group to throw the dice and then share their memories. At the end of this time allow the group to discuss things that were common to memories across the ages.

Source: Patrick Angier, in National and Diocesan Youth Network of the Church of England, *Youth A Part Resources Pack*

# Food

The story is often told of the great feast where everyone has to eat with five-foot chopsticks: in heaven everyone is well fed, but people starve in hell because they have not learnt to share and feed each other. Food is a great way to develop relationships. Instead of using five-foot chopsticks, try the following ideas.

## TASTE AND TALK

Everyone brings along food for a bring-and-share meal and sits around the display of food. No one is allowed to put food on to their own plate, only on to other people's. This exercise is usually enough to do in itself as people tend to concentrate on feeding each other. The atmosphere produced is conducive to ending with the peace and a meditation or prayer.

*or*

## SERVICE WITH A SMILE

The vicar and wardens/staff could cook and serve a meal for a group of young people and adults to eat together. Whilst the meal is being served and eaten the following questions could be used to facilitate discussion:

STARTERS!
1.   What food do you most enjoy?
2.   Where in the world would you most like to be?
3.   How would you spend £5,000?
4.   What is your favourite time of the year?

MAIN COURSE!
1.   How did you first get interested in Church?
2.   If you could compare yourself to an animal, which one would it be?
3.   What were your first or earliest impressions of Church?
4.   Who was the first best friend you can remember?
5.   Share a funny family story.
6.   Who is it you most admire?

DESSERT!
1.   Name the Bible character you feel you identify with most strongly.
2.   What do you think heaven is like?
3.   Talk about someone that you really trust.
4    Talk about a time when you felt let down.
5.   When was the best time of your life, so far?
6.   Who would you most like to be with in heaven?

Source: Patrick Angier, in National and Diocesan Youth Network of the Church of England, *Youth A Part Resources Pack* (adapted)

# Affirmation

Often the most significant influences on our lives are not events but people. People can influence our beliefs and ideals through to the core of our being. This exercise helps us to take a closer look at some of those people who have influenced us. It will work best in groups of about six people with a mixture of ages.

Place the following six statements on cards in the centre of the group.

| | | | | | |
|---|---|---|---|---|---|
| **1. Talk about one person who gave you an opportunity** | **2. Talk about one person who took a risk on you** | **3. Talk about one person who valued your abilities** | **4. Talk about one person who respected your views** | **5. Talk about one person who took an interest in your interests** | **6. Talk about one person who listened to you** |

When a group member wishes to speak about a certain card, he/she picks it up and talks. The rest of the group should then remain silent until the card has been replaced.

Source: Patrick Angier, in National and Diocesan Youth Network of the Church of England, *Youth A Part Resources Pack*

Photocopiable

# Light a candle

This activity could form part of an act of worship that involves all ages and is especially suitable for the close of the session.

Each person is given an unlit candle, and then a lighted candle is placed in the centre of the group. In silence, everyone has the opportunity to affirm other members of the group by lighting their own candle from the central one and then moving to light another person's candle. As they do this they can say something which will affirm, build up or show appreciation to the person they have chosen. This may be anything from 'I really enjoyed your company . . .', I thought what you said was . . .', to 'Thank you for . . .' After the candle has been lit, the person doing the lighting returns to his/her place and blows his/her own candle out. Throughout the exercise, the number of candles which are alight at any one time will fluctuate as some have to be blown out to affirm others whilst others are being lit from the central flame.

After this has continued for a while, end with a short silence and then a prayer or the Grace.

Source: Patrick Angier, in National and Diocesan Youth Network of the Church of England, *Youth A Part Resources Pack*

Photocopiable

The following questionnaire is designed for each young person to complete with a member of their family and return to the volunteer team for analysis and action.

## Family evaluation of our youth ministry

We firmly believe that our youth ministry should embrace the young person's family structure, by which we mean the group of people with whom each young person lives. This questionnaire will help us to see how we are doing, to evaluate how our youth ministry informs, involves and supports the families of its young people.

You will find two columns, one for the young person to fill in and one for a member of their family, i.e. the people with whom they live, to complete.

Please return the completed questionnaire to:

.................................................. by ....................................................

It will be read by ................................................. and action arising from your

responses will be shared with you in ..............................................................

1.   Do you feel that families get enough information about the youth ministry?
What do you like? What do you think we could improve?

**Young person:**                                    **Family member:**

2.   Do you feel that families are involved enough in the youth ministry's decision-making and planning? Are families given enough opportunities to get involved in supporting the ministry? What do you like? What do you think we could improve?

**Young person:**                                    **Family member:**

*(continued . . .)*

3.    Do you feel that families are supported enough in the youth ministry?
What do you like? What do you think we could improve?

**Young person:**                          **Family member:**

4.    Is there anything else that you feel the youth ministry should consider from a family's perspective?

**Young person:**                          **Family member:**

5.    Is there anything else you would like to tell us?

Age of young person:

Relationship of family member to young person:

Thank you!

## Summary

### The questions to ask:

- What are the family structures of our young people?

- How can our youth ministry embrace the young person's family?

- How can we
      inform
      involve
  and support the young people's families?

### Points for action:

- hold fifth meeting using the following **session outline**;

- hold a *Parent and child talking shop* using the **meeting outline** on page 64;

- hold a *Two-way support group* using the **meeting outline** on pages 63–64;

- implement appropriate consent forms (see Appendix 2) and share policies with parents.

### Useful resources:

- The Report of the Working Party of the Board for Social Responsibility, *Something to Celebrate – Valuing Families in Church*, Church House Publishing, 1995

- Your local FLAME (Family Life and Marriage Education) team

## Exploring youth ministry 5

## Session 5 outline

### Resources needed:

- flipchart and pens;

- Bible with passages marked;

- **group notes** copied as a handout for each person – these could be distributed prior to the meeting;

- **facilitator's notes** for the discussion facilitator;

- a copy of the **evaluation tool**, *Family evaluation of our youth ministry*, for each person (see pages 68–9).

### Prayer (5 minutes)

Read aloud Hebrews 2.10-13. Ask for God's blessing and guidance on the discussion and activity of the group.

### Opening Activity (15 minutes)

Give each person the *Parents' perspective questionnaire* and divide into small groups of four. Ask each group to answer the questions from the perspective of a parent of a young person. Give each group a different age of young person to 'parent' (include ages from 6 months to 30 years to ensure a broad cross-section of response). Bring the groups back together and ask each group to share their given age and responses.

### Discussion (55 minutes)

Ask someone in the group to act as 'scribe' if you feel it is appropriate.

The facilitator should lead the group through the discussion questions. A suggested timing is given which can be adapted to suit your church's needs.

### Summarizing and moving on (10 minutes)

Go through the discussion notes with the large group. Assign any action to be taken to members of the group and detail the deadline for completing the action. Ask for group consensus on the action list and note who will be responsible for distributing the lists and by when. Confirm arrangements for the next session.

## Prayer (5 minutes)

Read aloud Psalm 22.22-4. Say, 'Lord God, we thank you for our public meeting, for the chance to embrace your holy family through the family structures of our young people. Bless us as we seek to serve your family, heavenly Father. Amen.'

## Facilitator's notes

### What do we understand by the term family? (5 minutes)

Use the flipchart to list the different responses. Encourage the group fully to think through the different structures and relationships that can form a family.

### What are the family structures of our young people? (10 minutes)

This will require delicate attention to detail, to think through the structures both of the active and inactive young people in your church.

### How can our youth ministry embrace the young person's family? (15 minutes)

You may need to keep the group to the task here, it is easy to be theoretical, but you will need to move them on to practical steps to be taken as you answer the last question.

### How can we

### inform

### involve

### and support the young people's families?

(30 minutes)

Remember to be specific, realistic and detailed.

## Prayer

Listen to Hebrews 2.10-13. Ask for God's blessing and guidance on the discussion and activity of the group.

## Opening activity

In small groups, answer the questions on the *Parents' perspective questionnaire* in the next column from the perspective of a parent of a young person. Each group will be given a different age of young person to 'parent'.

As a large group share your responses.

## Questions for discussion

What do we understand by the term family?

What are the family structures of our young people?

How can our youth ministry embrace the young person's family?

How can we

inform

involve

and support the young people's families?

## Parents' perspective questionnaire

Please answer the following questions from the perspective of a parent of a ...-year-old.

- How does it feel to be a parent approaching the next millennium?

- What is one of your greatest concerns for your child?

- What is one of your greatest hopes for your child?

- What support would you like to receive as a parent?

- How do you think the youth ministry could support your family?

## Prayer

Listen to Psalm 22.22-4.

'Lord God, we thank you for our public meeting, for the chance to embrace your holy family through the family structures of our young people. Bless us as we seek to serve your family, heavenly Father. Amen.'

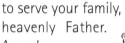

# 7 Young People and Worship

This is perhaps going to be the most frustrating chapter of all to read, because it offers a series of potentially difficult questions inviting you to consider existing worshippers' needs including those of your involved young people, non-involved young people's needs and the balancing of these alongside the possibilities for your church in terms of denominational policy, time, resources and, perhaps, your church history. Trying to effect this delicate balance requires a willingness to be vulnerable and to

**This chapter will ask you:**

✔ What are our young people's needs from worship?

✔ How does that fit in with our existing worship?

✔ How can the two come together?

take risks on behalf of the whole church and requires thorough preparation. Worship exploration is almost always an emotive issue in a church and when considering young people's needs can give rise to some of the biggest questions a church can face in developing a response to young people. Unfortunately, these do have to be thought through and answered by *your* church, because the decisions you make can only be determined by a common mind on behalf of your particular needs and situation.

# What are our young people's needs from worship?

Of course your young people are going to respond to this very differently depending on the shape of your particular youth ministry. If you have begun to develop a ministry of outreach to young people not connected with the church, then you will need to expose them to the possibilities of worship before they can respond. If your youth ministry is born out of a response to young people attending church as part of a family activity then they too may not feel sufficiently exposed to the varied options in worship, whilst a church that attracts a large independent body of young people – perhaps students at the local university – will have a body of young people who have chosen the church based on your style of worship and are likely to have experienced other styles and elements of worship and made a more deliberate choice. Whatever your local scenario, you are not going to be able to answer this question until you ask them.

Given the popularity of rock music, it is easy to assume that all young people will only want drum and guitar-led music. Many young people may well enjoy this, but assuming that this is the only provision you should make for them is limiting them and withholding the varied menu a church can offer.

The key elements to finding out what young people need from worship are to ensure that they have been exposed to a variety of worship styles and experiences and then get beyond what they are enjoying and find out why. Let us look a little more closely at each of these elements:

## Ensure that they have been exposed to a variety of worship styles and experiences

It may be that your church provides a menu of different services, perhaps a family service, Matins and a church Eucharist on a Sunday morning followed by a rotating programme of evening services – Taizé worship, praise services, choral evensong, Iona worship. Wonderful! But just because it's on offer doesn't mean that young

people will feel able to attend. To encourage them to try the different styles, why not offer a dedicated exploration – package meetings around each different service perhaps, offer a social programme and discussion after each evening service for a month, or switch your usual youth group night to a Sunday to include participation in different services? This doesn't mean being covert about your intentions; you will need the young people's approval before you make such plans and there will be some who don't feel able to attend the services. By offering them the opportunity to attend with the larger group in this way, the young people have the security of participating with other 'novices' as part of a comfortable community. The meeting afterwards offers them the chance to de-brief the experience, explore what they did and didn't respond to and why. Use the **evaluation tool** on page 76 for this discussion.

For many churches the resources to offer such a menu are just not available. This will mean slightly more preparation on behalf of the leaders and co-ordination of transport and venues, but it is still possible by using your denominational contacts. Find out what other churches are offering; perhaps there are some centrally offered services or even national events. Consult your denominational offices for details of local services.

## Get beyond what they are enjoying and find out why

With the best of intentions, it is easy to compartmentalize young people in worship. If, for example, we see a group of young people enjoying the drum and guitar-led music in a praise service, it is easy to assume that we need to put drums and guitars into every service in the hope that young people will attend. Of course many people of all ages enjoy such music in its own right, but we cannot assume that this is a compulsory ingredient. Young people are individuals with individual tastes and needs. It may be that young people find the praise service enjoyable because it is accessible; they may enjoy the more informal structure, the feelings of joy and celebration, feeling that they can wear more casual clothing or the timing or length of the service. All these elements are not exclusive to our hypothetical praise service, they can be offered in all forms of worship. This is in no way denying the value of the service; rather it is highlighting the fact that we should not compartmentalize young people. It is too easy to delight in finding something young people enjoy and thus limit their experience by not offering them complementary experiences. If a church seriously wants to involve young people in worship then it really needs to get behind the young people's reasons for the choices they make and respond directly to these.

## How does that fit in with our existing worship?

Once a dedicated period of research has been carried out, you will be prepared to begin to respond to this question. However, this is the point for one of the potentially biggest debates in youth ministry. Having identified the needs of your young people, how far are you prepared to go to meet them? How far do you feel you should have to go to meet them? These are not manipulative questions. In Chapter 2 we looked at the basic questions a church needs to ask itself at an initial meeting before developing a youth ministry. One of the key questions was whether you are an 'outside in' or 'inside out' church. Your response to this question will define how you respond to young people's needs in worship. If you take an 'outside in' approach then you will be familiar with offering activities shaped to suit young people and are likely to find the developing of worship that directly responds to their needs relatively straightforward. If you take an 'inside out' approach and develop young people's involvement within your existing worship then there are going to be more considerations for your church. This is not to say that either is a preferable option. It can be argued that an 'outside in' approach can deny young people the opportunity fully to experience your style of worship and potentially make them unable to commit to the church. A simple example of this might be an Anglican church offering on a

housing estate a youth service at which the Anglican creed is never included. The young person seeking to make a commitment could then potentially be confirmed within the Anglican church but be unprepared for the confirmation vows and commitment of beliefs that he or she would be making and feel unable to proceed. A church offering an 'outside in' approach needs to have thought through the follow-up it is prepared to make – will a young adult who outgrows a youth service be offered a 'next stage' in the same environment or will they then be expected to attend services at the church? This is obviously a wider question for the church to grapple with.

On the other hand a church offering an 'inside out' approach is going to have to consider its existing membership. If the young people express a need to feel accepted and comfortable within a Eucharist service but don't feel that the existing church Eucharist service meets this need, how is a church going to make this happen? If the answer is to adopt a more relaxed dress code and offer a variety of music, is the congregation ready to make this adaptation? Just because the need has been identified, are the existing congregation members going to know how to welcome young people? Is there going to be time for preparation and training for both age groups? Would there be attendance at a session on developing relationships across the age groups?

## How can the two come together?

It is now time to take some specific action. Have these discussions with the broadest possible cross-section of representation from your church. Revisit with those at the initial meeting your decisions on your approach to youth ministry and your mission statement. Make sure you have conducted research amongst the young people that informs those responsible for organizing worship as to the reasons young people enjoy and need specific elements of worship; then get going in preparing the church for the action. Consider a training session on inter-age relationship building. Ensure that everyone knows why new elements are being included in worship or a new service is being designed. Take time out of the service to explain, use notices and newsletters, offer people the chance to feed back and evaluate. The **evaluation tool** included below will be useful both in asking young people to respond to their needs in worship and also as a device to get feedback when new initiatives are introduced. Even if you are not following the session outlines,

you may like to use the evaluation tool as an exercise in inter-age discussion.

The exercise described is designed to enable everyone in the group to speak and contribute to a meaningful discussion. This can be used after attendance at a new service of worship. Whilst this exercise looks at the service the group has just attended, its format can be used for de-briefing or discussing any group experience.

## Evaluation tool

### Ask the group to sit comfortably in a circle.

Circles allow everyone to see one another and make it easy for participants to know when it's their turn to speak. If you are going to have to make notes to report back to a planning group, for example, explain this to the group and make the notes on a flipchart so everyone can see what is being recorded.

### Ask each person in turn to say one thing they didn't enjoy about the service.

Starting with the group leader, this allows everyone to contribute something, no matter how trivial or unsubstantiated. Once each person has spoken in this way, their confidence will have increased to feel able to speak again later if there is something they want to say.

When everyone has spoken, summarize the things that weren't enjoyed by the group and ask them if they can expand on why they think each thing didn't work. This is open discussion and the group leader will need to keep the group disciplined to speak one at a time and encourage them to say specifically why they think something didn't work. As you draw these questions to a close, ask if there is anyone who hasn't said anything who would like to. Sum up the conclusions drawn.

### Ask each person in turn to say one thing they enjoyed about the service.

By putting this question second the discussion can end on a more positive note. Summarize the things that were enjoyed by the group and ask them if they can expand on why they think each thing worked.

### Finally:

Ask the group if there is anything else they would like to say. If you have used a flipchart, re-read the notes made and ask for group consensus that they are an accurate record or reflection of the discussion.

Thank the group for their contributions.

Photocopiable

## Summary

### The questions to ask:

- What are our young people's needs from worship?

- How does that fit in with our existing worship?

- How can the two come together?

### Points for action:

- hold sixth meeting using the following **session outline**;

- conduct a dedicated period of research of services as detailed in the chapter;

- ask these difficult questions of the church.

### Useful resources:

- George Carey, *Spiritual Journey*, Mowbrays, 1994

- S. Heathfield, *Rave On*, CPAS, 1995

- Patrick Angier, *Changing Youth Worship*, National Society/Church House Publishing, 1998

## Exploring youth ministry 6

## Session 6 outline

### Resources needed:

- flipchart and pens;

- music and accompaniment for singing (remember tape recorder if needed);

- **group notes** copied as a handout for each person – these could be distributed prior to the meeting;

- **facilitator's notes** for the discussion facilitator;

- a copy of the **evaluation tool** from page 76 for the discussion facilitator.

### Prayer (5 minutes)

Offer a short period for personal reflection. Close by saying 'Lord God, we come to you prepared for what might be a very difficult discussion. We ask for your help and guidance through the session and ask for an openness of heart and a listening ear. Amen.'

### Opening activity (10 minutes)

Use this time to sing a variety of different hymns and worship songs – make sure you have at least six completely different songs to sing, representative of different worship styles. If your group is large enough, you will need only the accompaniment of piano or guitar as available and appropriate. If you are quite a small group a confident leader and/or a recording of the music will increase volume and thus confidence at joining in. Enjoy the experience for its own sake.

### Discussion (60 minutes)

Ask someone in the group to act as 'scribe' if you feel it is appropriate.

The facilitator should lead the group through the discussion questions. A suggested timing is given which can be adapted to suit your church's needs.

### Summarizing and moving on (10 minutes)

Go through the discussion notes with the large group. Assign any action to be taken to members of the group and detail the deadline for completing the action. Ask for group consensus on the action list and note who will be responsible for distributing the lists and by when. Confirm arrangements for the next session.

### Prayer (5 minutes)

Again offer a time for silent reflection. Ask the group to stand in a circle and give thanks for each other by saying, 'Lord, we thank you for our chance to be a group. We give thanks for each and every one of us and the varied experiences we bring to the group. We are now going to give thanks for each other by naming out loud the person on our right, each of us speaking in turn. I'll start: Lord, thank you for . . . Amen.'

## Facilitator's notes

### What are our young people's needs from worship? (15 minutes)

You will need to have conducted the research as outlined in this chapter and have both heard from young people as to how they responded and got behind why they responded in this way. If you have time, you could use the discussion outline given in the **evaluation tool** within this meeting. As always, this is not a time for speculation on behalf of the adults; ensure you have young people's feedback to present.

### How does that fit in with our existing worship? (20 minutes)

Be prepared for intense discussion in response to these two questions, allow time for emotional responses, but ensure that practical steps are outlined. Chairing this part of the discussion will require sensitive, positive facilitating on your part.

### How can the two come together? (25 minutes)

You will need to move the group to decisive points for action here, pulling together the feedback from the young people and the emotional responses into specific steps to be taken. Why not summarize this section with an action list, detailing responsible individuals and deadlines for each step?

## Exploring youth ministry 6

### Prayer

After a short period of personal reflection:

'Lord God, we come to you prepared for, what might be, a very difficult discussion. We ask for your help and guidance through the session and ask for an openness of heart and a listening ear. Amen.'

### Questions for discussion

What are our young people's needs from worship?

How does that fit in with our existing worship?

How can the two come together?

### Prayer

After a time of silent reflection, stand in a circle and give thanks for each other by saying, 'Lord, we thank you for our chance to be a group. We give thanks for each and every one of us and the varied experiences we bring to the group. We are now going to give thanks for each other by naming out loud the person on our right, each of us speaking in turn. Lord, thank you for . . . Amen.'

### Opening activity

During this time we will sing a variety of different hymns and worship songs. Enjoy the experience!

# Peer Ministry

## What?

The term 'peer ministry' is widely understood to describe ministry initiatives delivered by young people on behalf of other young people. This concept of a youth-initiated and youth-led ministry can only be thought of as a good thing, as it ultimately promotes youth ownership of youth ministry. However, it is not an easy concept to grapple with and any church wishing to embrace the notion and, ultimately, the reality of peer ministry must be prepared for some of the issues it raises.

### This chapter will help you:

✔ exploit the philosophy of your ministry;

✔ consider when and why peer ministry can fail;

✔ begin to develop your own peer ministry initiative.

## How?

Successful peer ministry takes time and intense dedication to establish. Its concept and philosophy need to be embraced by the whole church. For young people to acquire the skills and experiences needed successfully to execute peer ministry requires an environment in which they can be allowed to attempt, fail or succeed, grow from that experience and attempt again. This inevitably involves a huge amount of risk on behalf of the church. Such risk is only possible to take if the church has embraced all of its possible ramifications and is prepared to stand alongside the young people in their attempt.

We have already explored how to involve young people in the decision-making process and acknowledged that their involvement in all of the preparation is paramount if a ministry is going to succeed. Peer ministry is, in its essence, much more than consultation with young people about their ministry, it is rather their direct ownership and delivery of that ministry.

Peer ministry is a stepped process. Its ultimate aim is enabling young people to lead themselves and others spiritually. A youth ministry may develop to allow some of its participants naturally to form a core group with the potential for peer leadership. Peer ministry is a natural, though not inevitable, development of youth ministry. Peer ministry cannot be imposed onto a youth ministry.

Let us take an example of one church with which I worked:

> *I was happily told that the church was involving young people by having two under-16-year-old members on their PCC. Of an elected body of nine, this seemed a positive step forward and indeed the church were proud of the young people's involvement. When I attended a PCC meeting, I found that Darren (aged 16) and Sam (aged 14) were indeed present at the meeting but seemed to take no part in its discussions or decision-making. When they were asked a question, it was of such magnitude that they felt unable to respond. For example, 'How do young people feel about coming to church?' and 'Why aren't more young people joining the priesthood?' Darren and Sam felt unable to speak on their own behalf, let alone on behalf of their entire generation.*

> *This particular church had involved Darren and Sam in all good faith. They had thought about the lack of young people's involvement and had done something about it. However, members were*

> *disappointed about Darren and Sam's lack of contribution at meetings and involvement in the church. They had hoped that Darren and Sam would take on the responsibility for getting members of their peer group involved in church life, possibly even starting a youth group for themselves.*

Unfortunately the church had not done enough:

1.   They had not thought through how to equip Darren and Sam with the information needed to 'survive' PCC meetings and empower them to contribute to the proceedings. The PCC meeting was conducted in what, to Darren and Sam, seemed like a foreign language. Clearly no-one had offered them explanations as to the procedure at the meetings or some of the 'jargon' in which the meeting was conducted. Several members of the PCC were very vocal whilst several remained relatively silent, thus Darren and Sam were unable to take a cue as to when it would be appropriate to contribute.

2.   Furthermore, Darren's and Sam's involvement on the PCC was misplaced. The church's agenda was to have young people involved more in the life of the church. However, a PCC is a leadership body, and consequently Darren and Sam were inadvertently placed in the role of being leaders regardless of whether or not they were equipped to do so. The church had thus imposed a peer ministry onto the young people, before a youth ministry had been established.

# Where are we going?

**Core of excited Christians**

– peer ministry
– outreach

**Service**

– peer ministry training
– initiatives in city

**Challenge of faith**

– growth of sharing in group discussion
– need to share faith with leaders

**Lightbulb – relationship with Jesus**

– recognition of worship with Jesus

**Group enjoys being community**

– experience and community – enjoy being together, survive highs and lows
– at youth group meetings begin to share non-threatening thoughts and information

**Social fun**

– relational ministry of welcome – fun, social, non-threatening

Source: Institute for Professional Youth Ministry (adapted)

Photocopiable

# Where are we going?

Look at the diagram on page 82. In this diagram we can see how a youth ministry can develop from the foundation of relational ministry through to a natural core group of young people with the desire to learn the skills to develop relationships with other young people: in other words, peer ministry. The diagram represents a series of steps of potential growth for young people. What is important is to recognize that:

- not all young people will wish to climb all the steps;

- participants can stay on one step for their entire involvement in youth ministry. The steps are not a process of elimination — there is room for everyone on every step but it is likely that only some will take all of the steps;

- group dynamics might mean that the group travels up and down the steps as changes occur or a new influx of members arrive. It is important to recognize that this is alright and perfectly normal.

If your church is addressing youth ministry with the help of this book because young people have recognized a need for youth ministry provision and have sought the help of the church, then you already have peer ministry in action. However, the more common scenario is of adult concern combined with awareness of young people's needs and hopes inspiring action for youth ministry provision. It may take two, ten or twenty years to come to a point of readiness for a peer ministry initiative. What is important is that it is needs driven and not imposed. With either model the church can help by providing support in the developing and training of leadership and by being fully prepared for the risks involved.

The church can prepare itself by asking the following questions:

- What do we understand peer ministry to be? How do we respond to the concept?

- What do we understand by leadership? How do we respond to the notion of leadership?

- What kind of peer ministry initiative could we offer? What preparatory training should we offer?

## The notion of leadership

It is worth noting that many find the word 'leader' difficult because it can conjure up the image of somebody with all the answers 'leading' those without the answers the right way. This is an important exploration for a church, rather than assuming that you all share the same view, not least because when we talk about young people being in roles of leadership it can be a stumbling block for many to see peer ministry as selecting the chosen young people to have the right answers which they can then impart to those without them. The word leader is used in this book really for want of a better word and to convey an enabler, organizer, up-front person, chair and person responsible for getting the group going. The understanding is that leadership is a gift of the Spirit.

Take time to allow people to explore their feelings about youth leadership and ensure that people understand that any leadership training is open to all young people to attend, rather than by invitation for a chosen minority. Leaders may, of course, wish to encourage more reticent young people to get involved but should never hand-pick a select few.

## What kind of peer ministry initiative could we offer? What preparatory training should we offer?

Examples of a peer ministry initiative might include a school outreach programme, leadership of a particular youth group, pastoral and prayerful teams at worship services or the running of a youth service. The table overleaf shows how appropriate training might be offered for these particular initiatives:

# Training

| Initiative | Training needed |
|---|---|
| Prayer and pastoral team at worship services | 1. listening skills<br>2. prayer resources<br>3. developing a team approach<br>4. knowing when and how to refer<br>5. using a mentor/spiritual director<br>6. exploring experiences and understanding of this role |
| Youth group leadership | 1. planning skills<br>2. leading activities<br>3. knowledge of resources<br>4. developing a team approach<br>5. knowing when to lead and when to listen<br>6. leadership styles<br>7. *Good Practice* guidelines and implications |
| Youth service | 1. worship leading<br>2. resources<br>3. developing a theme in worship<br>4. planning and preparation |
| One-to-one peer mentoring | 1. the role of a mentor<br>2. mentoring skills<br>3. developing appropriate relationships<br>4. maintaining boundaries<br>5. listening skills<br>6. prayer resources<br>7. knowing when and how to refer |
| Youth outreach programme | 1. identifying 'target' areas/groups<br>2. developing a strategy<br>3. planning skills<br>4. knowledge of resources<br>5. follow-up preparation<br>6. evaluation techniques |

There are ready-to-use training resources available as well as human resources. Once again your denominational youth officer will be able to help direct you to such resources. Although the examples of peer ministry initiatives given above pertain to a Christian setting, the statutory youth sector has long been involved in peer education and leadership and many local authorities and youth agencies will be able to support you and may even have peripatetic peer educators willing to visit groups at their invitation. One rural benefice I worked with linked up with the Local Authority youth worker to join their peer education programme and offered 'bolt-on' modules for the Christian elements of their initiative. Interestingly, such fellowship had developed amongst the group that *all* the young people took the extra modules.

Whatever approach your church takes, it is important that delivery of training is professional and appropriate. Remember to involve young people in the delivery of the training too.

# Evaluation tool

On page 86 overleaf is a questionnaire adapted from the book *Kids Taking Charge: Youth-led Youth Ministry*. Why not use the questionnaire as a launching point for discussion with the members before the initiative is established? Once active, the questionnaire can be used as a method of evaluation with the members of the group and the leadership team.

This questionnaire can be used with adults – church council members, volunteer team members, parents – to help assess whether the adults in the church community are ready for the risks involved in supporting a peer ministry initiative. The results should be collated and used to assess the readiness of the church. If the analysis shows a lack of readiness, then the planning team will be able to see what training and preparation needs to be offered to the church to enable them fully to support the peer ministry.

## Summary

### The questions to ask:

- What do we understand peer ministry to be? How do we respond to the concept?

- What do we understand by leadership? How do we respond to the notion of leadership?

- What kind of peer ministry initiative could we offer? What preparatory training should we offer?

### Points for action:

- hold seventh meeting using the **session outline** on page 89;

## Useful resources:

- Thom and Joani Schultz, *Kids Taking Charge: Youth-led Youth Ministry*, Group Books, Colorado, 1991

- Your Local Authority Youth Service – Peer Education Projects

- John Buckeridge, *Nurturing Young Disciples*, Marshall Pickering, 1996

- *How Faith Grows*, National Society/ Church House Publishing, 1991

- C. M. Shelton, *Adolescent Spirituality*, Crossroad, New York, 1983

# My evaluation of our church's youth ministry right now

## A My perception of youth ministry ownership

Our church's youth ministry is *best* described as . . . (tick one)

_____ *my* youth ministry.
_____ *their* youth minstry.
_____ *our* youth ministry.

Give three reasons why you feel that way:

1. _____
2. _____
3. _____

If your answers reflect a 'me, mine, I' or 'their, them, they' flavour, your youth ministry could be struggling with an ownership problem. Words such as 'ours, we, us' portray a 'we're-in-this-together' attitude. Youth-based ministry can promote that togetherness approach.

## B My perception of youth ministry responsibility

Circle the response you feel best reflects your church's youth ministry:

1. Young people carry out their responsibility.                                  always/sometimes/never

2. Adults carry out their responsibility.                                        always/sometimes/never

3. Group members take a great deal of ownership in the youth ministry.           always/sometimes/never

4. Young people are involved in planning our programmes and activities.          always/sometimes/never

5. Young people are involved in leading our programmes and activities.           always/sometimes/never

6. Young people provide high visibility for the church's youth ministry.         always/sometimes/never

7. The congregation views young people as valuable members of the church.        always/sometimes/never

8. The same people do all the work in our youth ministry.                        always/sometimes/never

9. Our programmes offer young people an opportunity to grow
   in responsibility and leadership.                                             always/sometimes/never

Answering 'always' or 'sometimes' for all the statements except 8 shows you're already involved in youth-based ministry to some degree. When youth-based ministry begins to fly, statement 8 changes from the 'same people doing all the work' to 'a variety of young people and adults making ministry happen.'

(continued . . .)

## C  My perception of our youth ministry structure

Circle which diagram best represents your youth group's leadership structure right now:

**1. Military model**    **2. Representative model**    **3. Group process model**

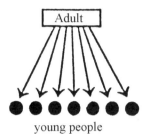

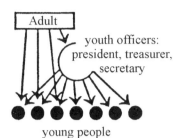

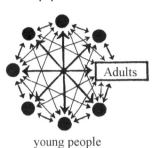

(For a more detailed explanation of each model, see page 55.)

If you did not circle 'group process model', what impact would a change to this model have on your present ministry?

If you did circle 'group process model', what are: your frustrations with the model? your joys?

Youth ministry can happen under each structure pictured above. But the benefits of youth-based ministry occur when a group practises the group process. Both the military and representative models have their place under certain circumstances. But for the greatest growth, ownership and shared-leadership responsibility, the intricate web work of group interaction works best.

You'll need to take a closer look at the other models and see where you currently feel most comfortable. Or, to see where you'll need to grow.

The following evaluations will help you do that.


## D  My perception of the purpose of our youth ministry

Youth ministry exists in our church for the purpose of: (tick all that apply.)

_____ evangelizing young people.

_____ deepening young people's faith.

_____ meeting young people's needs.

_____ helping young people grow.

_____ attracting whole families into the congregation through high youth visibility.

_____ involving young people in the life of the church.

_____ teaching healthy values to teenagers.

_____ providing an avenue for young people to express their gifts.

_____ giving young people a chance to serve.

_____ other: _____

*(continued . . .)*

Our present organizational structure is in place because it: (tick all that apply)

_____ accomplishes the above goals.

_____ benefits the young people.

_____ makes my job easier.

_____ has always been done that way.

_____ has never been thought about in any other way.

_____ provides visibility for young people.

_____ provides visibility for me.

_____ pleases the 'powers that be.'

_____ other: _____

Youth-based ministry strives to meet the needs and to fulfil the purpose of the group through framework. Does your present organizational structure help accomplish the youth ministry's goals and benefit young people? If you're uncertain, it might be time for a youth ministry make-over.

## E  My connection and contribution to our youth ministry right now

Place an 'X' on each line in the 'Me-O-Meter' showing what best describes your leadership style right now.

**ME-O-METER**

| Hurrah! There's no problem. | Help! There's a problem. |

When it comes to . . .

1.  delegating and giving away responsibility, I feel . . .

2.  needing to be up front, I feel . . .

3.  needing to be in total control, I feel . . .

4.  needing to have things run perfectly, I feel . . .

5.  needing to have the senior clergy and the congregation see me in control, I feel . . .

Source: Thom and Joani Schultz, *Kids Taking Charge* (adapted)

## Exploring youth ministry 7

## Session 7 outline

### Resources needed:

- flipchart and pens;

- Bible with passages marked;

- a chosen blessing for the closing prayer;

- **group notes** copied as a handout for each person – these could be distributed prior to the meeting;

- **facilitator's notes** for the discussion facilitator;

- a copy of the questionnaire used as an **evaluation tool** for each person.

### Prayer (5 minutes)

Read aloud Luke 14.25-33. Allow time for personal reflection on the tower being built in the youth ministry and for the costing and foundation-laying being carried out in this meeting.

### Opening activity (10 minutes)

Ask the group to sit in a circle; if your group is very large you may need to divide into smaller groups. Ask members to take it in turns to share the story of how they were given their Christian name, who chose it, whether they have had any nicknames, whether or not they like their names.

### Discussion (60 minutes)

Ask someone in the group to act as 'scribe' if you feel it is appropriate.

The facilitator should lead the group through the discussion questions. A suggested timing is given which can be adapted to suit your church's needs.

### Summarizing and moving on (10 minutes)

Go through the discussion notes with the large group. Assign any action to be taken to members of the group and detail the deadline for completing the action. Ask for group consensus on the action list and note who will be responsible for distributing the lists and by when. Confirm arrangements for the next session.

### Prayer (5 minutes)

Close with a blessing of your choosing and a prayer of thanksgiving for the work done in this meeting.

## Facilitator's notes

### What do we understand peer ministry to be? How do we respond to the concept? (15 minutes)

Use the flipchart to list key words and phrases. Then divide the flipchart sheet into two columns, one side titled 'The case for' the other 'The case against'. List people's responses accordingly.

### What do we understand by leadership? How do we respond to the notion of leadership? (10 minutes)

Allow time for sensitive exploration and discussion.

### What kind of peer ministry initiative should we offer? What preparatory training should we offer? (35 minutes)

Encourage the group to be realistic. If you have invited an outside speaker, such as your denominational youth officer or a peer education specialist, you will need to adapt the session to accommodate them at this point. As always, detail specific action and attribute the person responsible.

# Exploring youth ministry 7

## Prayer

Listen to Luke 14.25-33.

During the time of personal reflection focus on the tower being built in the youth ministry and for the costing and foundation-laying being carried out in this meeting.

## Opening activity

Sitting in a circle, you will be asked to take it in turns to share the story of how you were given your Christian name, who chose it, whether you have had any nicknames, whether or not you like your names.

## Questions for discussion

What do we understand peer ministry to be? How do we respond to the concept?

What do we understand by leadership? How do we respond to the notion of leadership?

What kind of peer ministry initiative should we offer? What preparatory training should we offer?

## Prayer

The session will close with a blessing and a prayer of thanksgiving for the work done in this meeting.

# Ongoing Youth Ministry

## Ongoing evaluation

As we have seen throughout this book, every stage of a developing ministry needs evaluation. It also needs acknowledgement and direct response to the evaluation. In each of the last chapters, a different **evaluation tool** has been offered to help you evaluate each area.

What is also crucial to the life of any youth ministry is ongoing evaluation of the whole ministry, looking at the broader picture of youth ministry and cross-referencing needs, joys, concerns and points for action. Evaluation should not happen only occasionally or just in the early stages, but as a regular part of church life. Such a frame of

### This chapter will help you to ask:

✔ How are we doing?

✔ Are we fulfilling our mission statement?

✔ What do we need to do next?

reference allows the youth ministry to remain a full part of the church's life, preventing a feeling of isolation for those involved and enabling the whole congregation to feel involved with the ministry.

An ongoing programme of evaluation will also present a professional approach to youth ministry and will encourage people to get involved, seeing that they are supported by the church family.

By now you will have a responsible body for the oversight of your youth ministry: perhaps it rests with the church council, perhaps with a designated committee. This chapter offers you a final

**evaluation tool** to enable you to poll the views of your whole church community. The **session outline** is based on the findings of this evaluation and can be used by the whole church at a dedicated meeting, by those following the **session outlines** as an eight-part course, or by the group responsible for the oversight of your youth ministry. Use the **evaluation tool** to poll everyone in your church – get the views of all the people represented at your initial church meeting:

> children
>
> young people and young adults in their 20s and 30s
>
> adults in their 40s, 50s, 60s, 70s, 80s, 90s
>
> families
>
> parents and grandparents
>
> single people
>
> couples without children
>
> those working with existing children's and youth groups
>
> attached uniformed organizations
>
> new members of the congregation
>
> more established members of the congregation
>
> members from congregations of your different services

However, the review of the youth ministry should not be a one-off. Such evaluation and review is paramount to the success of the ministry and should happen regularly, frequently enough to have an impact on the ministry but not so often as to make it seem irrelevant. As with the youth ministry itself, you will know how and when it is appropriate to review, evaluate and take action to move on.

## Celebration and affirmation

The journey you will have travelled to this point is really worth celebrating; whether you have managed to get all those you listed in Chapter 1 to read this book or you have established some of the initiatives you had planned as a church, take time to take stock of your achievements. Give yourself a breather as a church, celebrate what you have done, ensure that everyone in the church has a chance to catch up with what you have achieved and to share in the celebrations. So often as a church we are so busy 'doing', that we don't allow ourselves time to acknowledge how far we have travelled. By carving out specific times for acknowledgement and celebration, we enable each other to be affirmed and thanked, to delight in each other and each other's ministry and allow ourselves to approach evaluation as a positive, constructive experience. Here are some suggestions to engage your church in a confidence-raising, spiritually uplifting, affirming celebration of your youth ministry journey:

- hold the eighth **session outline** within the context of a party;

- throw a separate party purely as a celebration;

- set aside one Sunday as a youth ministry celebration – use this as a theme for your services; bring the volunteer team forward in the service to give public thanks for their ministry, ask the young people to deliver the sermon concentrating on the importance of youth ministry; hold a youth service; hold a church family lunch to celebrate and offer an all-age, open youth-group meeting;

- launch a youth ministry newsletter that highlights youth ministry activities and issues;

- offer a special feature in the church magazine and/or local newspaper on the youth ministry;

- write individual thank-you notes to all those involved in the establishing of the youth ministry response;

- take a church away-day focusing on the youth ministry, use it both to focus on the evaluation and to offer a time of celebration and thanksgiving;

- set up an inter-age prayer and affirmation partner initiative;

- invite a speaker or workshop leader from a specialist youth agency to come and inspire and affirm the church.

## Evaluation

When distributing the questionnaire that follows on page 94, attach a covering letter explaining your review process, who you have asked to respond and why, who will read the responses and how the results of the evaluation will be shared with the church. You will know what is appropriate to include for your church.

## Summary

### The questions to ask:
- How are we doing?
- Are we fulfilling our mission statement?
- What do we need to do next?

### Points for action:
- hold **eighth** meeting using the **session outline** on page 97;
- offer the church a chance to celebrate the achievements and development of the ministry so far;
- hold the cross-church evaluation (refer to your initial church meeting).

### Useful resources:
- National and Diocesan Youth Network of the Church of England, *Youth A Part Resources Pack*, National Society / Church House Publishing, 1996

### Ongoing reading:
- Peter Brierley, *Reaching and Keeping Teenagers*, MARC, Monarch Publications, 1993

- K. Ford, *Jesus for a New Generation*, Hodder & Stoughton, 1995

- L. J. Francis and W. K. Kay, *Teenage Religion and Values*, Redwood Books, Trowbridge, 1995

- L. J. Kay, W. K. Kerbey et al., *Fast Moving Currents in Youth Culture*, Lynx Communications, 1995

- J. P. Leighton, *The Principles and Practice of Youth and Community Work*, Chester House Publications, 1972

# Our youth ministry's mission statement is:

## How well do you think we are fulfilling this in terms of:

*(Please answer all those questions you can by circling the appropriate number)*

|  | Not at all | | | | | | | | | Completely |
|---|---|---|---|---|---|---|---|---|---|---|

**Our volunteer team**          1 2 3 4 5 6 7 8 9 10

*Please give reasons*

**Relationships across
the youth ministry**          1 2 3 4 5 6 7 8 9 10

*Please give reasons*

**Organized groups and meetings**   1 2 3 4 5 6 7 8 9 10

*Please give reasons*

**Our approach to families**      1 2 3 4 5 6 7 8 9 10

*Please give reasons*

**Worship**              1 2 3 4 5 6 7 8 9 10

*Please give reasons*

**Peer ministry initiatives**      1 2 3 4 5 6 7 8 9 10

*Please give reasons*

*(continued . . .)*

Photocopiable

## Do you feel that the youth ministry is:

holistic? Why / why not?

part of the church? Why / why not?

appropriate for our church? Why / why not?

## What do you most enjoy about the youth ministry?

*(Please give reasons)*

## What do you struggle with in the youth ministry?

*(Please give reasons)*

## What would you like to see the youth ministry do more of?

*(Please give reasons)*

## Are there any other comments you would like to make?

## Is there any aspect of the youth ministry where you could offer support?

*(If so, please include details here along with your name and address so that we can get in touch with you)*

*(continued . . .)*

## Please let us know whether you are:

*(Please tick* all *that apply)*

- ❑ A young person age_____
- ❑ An adult age: (circle the range that applies) 20s, 30s, 40s, 50s, 60s, 70s and over
- ❑ Involved in a youth group
- ❑ No longer involved in a youth group
- ❑ A member of the volunteer team
- ❑ A member of the church council
- ❑ A member of the group responsible for the oversight of the youth ministry
- ❑ A parent
- ❑ A guardian
- ❑ A grandparent
- ❑ An adult with no children
- ❑ Involved in the children's ministry of the church
- ❑ A long-standing member of the church community
- ❑ A new member of the church community
- ❑ A new member of the church community who joined this church because of the active youth ministry

*Thank you for your time!*

## Exploring youth ministry 8

## Session 8 outline

Why not consider holding this session as part of a party of celebration for all that you have achieved so far? Offer food and time to enjoy each other's company and to celebrate!

### Resources needed:

- flipchart with opening activity questions and pens for recording responses;

- things needed for communion (if to be used);

- **group notes** copied as a handout for each person – these could be distributed prior to the meeting;

- **facilitator's notes** for the discussion facilitator;

- a copy of the questionnaire used as an **evaluation tool** for each person;

- collated responses to the questionnaire, displayed or distributed to the group.

### Prayer (5 minutes)

This would be an ideal time for a house communion, obviously extending your meeting time to allow for the communion. If this is inappropriate for your church, then open with time for personal reflection on the youth ministry and the work of the group during these sessions.

### Opening activity (10 minutes)

Ask those gathered to pair up with someone they do not know well. Ask them to find out from their partner the answers to the following questions:

What is your name?

What is one thing you have enjoyed from being part of this group?

What is one thing that no-one else in this room knows about you?

What is one hope you have for the youth ministry?

Bring the group back to a circle and ask each person to introduce their partner to the rest of the group and share their answers to these questions.

### Discussion (55 minutes)

Ask someone in the group to act as 'scribe' if you feel it is appropriate.

The facilitator should lead the group through the responses to the questionnaire and summarize as a record on the flipchart. The facilitator will need to lead the group to decide on realistic steps to take next and to detail specific action to be taken.

### Summarizing and moving on (10 minutes)

Go through the discussion notes with the large group. Assign any action to be taken to members of the group and detail the deadline for completing the action. Ask for group consensus on the action list and note who will be responsible for distributing the lists and by when. Confirm arrangements for any follow-up meeting.

### Prayer (10 minutes)

Ask the group to stand in a circle and give thanks for each other by saying, 'Lord, we thank you for our chance to be a group. We give thanks for each and every one of us and our varied experiences we have brought to the group. We are now going to give thanks for each other by naming out loud the person on our right and for one particular thing we have enjoyed about that person, each of us speaking in turn. I'll start: Lord, thank you for . . . and for his/her gift of . . . Amen.'

## Facilitator's notes

Use the questionnaire as the basis for your discussion, either looking at each as a whole group, or looking at the collated responses in smaller groups before feeding back. You will need to be firm with time!

## Exploring youth ministry 8

### Prayer

The session will open with a time of prayer and reflection.

### Opening activity

You will be asked to pair up with someone you do not know well. Find out from your partner the answers to the following questions:

What is your name?

What is one thing you have enjoyed from being part of this group?

What is one thing that no-one else in this room knows about you?

What is one hope you have for the youth ministry?

In the large group, introduce your partner to the rest of the group and share their answers to these questions.

### Discussion

We will use the responses to the questionnaire as the basis for our discussion.

### Prayer

The group will stand in a circle and give thanks for each other by saying, 'Lord, we thank you for our chance to be a group. We give thanks for each and every one of us and our varied experiences we have brought to the group. We are now going to give thanks for each other by naming out loud the person on our right and for one particular thing we have enjoyed about that person, each of us speaking in turn. 'Lord thank you for . . . and for his/her gift of . . . Amen'.

# Safe from harm

## Summary of recommendations

In order to safeguard the welfare of the children and young people in their charge, voluntary organizations should consider the issues raised by each of the following statements of principle and then, if they wish to do so, take any action which they deem to be appropriate in the light of their circumstances and structures, and the nature of their activities:

1. Adopt a policy statement on safeguarding the welfare of children.

2. Plan the work of the organization so as to minimize situations where the abuse of children may occur.

3. Introduce a system whereby children may talk with an independent person.

4. Apply agreed procedures for protecting children to all paid staff and volunteers.

5. Give all paid staff and volunteers clear roles.

6. Use supervision as a means of protecting children.

7. Treat all would-be paid staff and volunteers as job applicants for any position involving contact with children.

8. Gain at least one reference from a person who has experience of the applicant's paid work or volunteering with children.

9. Explore all applicants' experience of working or contact with children in an interview before appointment.

10. Find out whether an applicant has any conviction for criminal offences against children.

11. Make paid and voluntary appointments conditional on the successful completion of a probationary period.

12. Issue guidelines on how to deal with the disclosure or discovery of abuse.

13. Train paid staff and volunteers, their line managers or supervisors, and policy makers in the prevention of child abuse.

Source: David R. Smith, *Safe from Harm*, copyright © Crown and reproduced with the permission of the Controller of Her Majesty's Stationery Office

# General information and consent

Church:

Group:

Full Name:

Details of any regular medication, medical problem (e.g. asthma, diabetes, allergies, dietary needs) or disability which may affect normal activity:

Address:

Name of parent/guardian:

Daytime telephone number:

Evening telephone number:

Name of additional contact (grandparent, etc.):

Telephone number:

I give permission for:

to take part in the normal activities of this group. I understand that separate permission will be sought for certain activities, including swimming and outings lasting longer than the normal meeting times of the group.

Signature of parent or guardian:

Date:

This form *should be filled in annually* and then retained in your group's records.

# Activities and day visits

Proposed visit or activity:

**Design your own form to include the following:**

- name of visit or activity;
- date;
- venue/destination;
- departure place and time;
- return place and time;
- cost (inc. cheque payable to . . . );
- transport arrangments;
- items to be brought (swimming kit, packed lunch, money, etc. . . . );
- date by which reply is to be made, and person to whom it should be sent.

**Then, include in your form a photocopy of the reply slip below.**

------------------------------------------------------------------------------------------------

REPLY SLIP                  ONE FORM PER PERSON

Full name of young person:

Address:

Telephone number for emergencies:
Daytime:

Evening:

Please give details of any medical conditions (e.g. asthma, diabetes, allergies or dietary needs) or disability that may be affected by this activity:

I have read the above information and I give permission for:

to participate fully in this activity.
or I give permission for:

to go with the group but not to participate in:

I give my consent to any medical treatment that may be necessary in event of emergency.
I enclose a cheque or cash to the sum of:

Signature of parent or guardian:

Date:

This consent form should be taken with the worker on the activity or visit.

This sheet may be photocopied.

Source: *Worth Doing Well*, Methodist Publishing House, copyright © Trustees for Methodist Church Purposes

# Hazardous activities

---

Proposed visit or activity:

---

Design your own form to include the following:

- name of site or activity;

   This must state clearly: *the exact nature of any hazardous activity to be undertaken, the ratio of workers to young people, the person responsible for the activity and their qualifications.*
- date;
- venue/destination;

- departure place and time;
- return place and time;
- cost (inc. cheque payable to . . . );
- transport arrangements;
- items to be brought (swimming kit, packed lunch, money, etc. . . . );
- date by which reply is to be made, and person to whom it should be sent.

**Then, include in your form a photocopy of the reply slip below.**

---

REPLY SLIP                                                    ONE FORM PER PERSON

---

Full name of young person:

Address:

---

Telehone number for emergencies:
Daytime:

Evening:

---

Please give details of any medical conditions (e.g. asthma, diabetes, allergies or dietary needs) or disability that may be affected by this activity:

---

I have read the above information and I give permission for:

to participate fully in this activity.
or I give permission for:

to go with the group but not to participate in:

I give my consent to any medical treatment that may be necessary in event of emergency.
I enclose a cheque or cash to the sum of:

Signature of parent or guardian:

Date:

---

This consent form should be taken with the worker on the activity or visit.

This sheet may be photocopied.
Source: *Worth Doing Well,* Methodist Publishing House, copyright © Trustees for Methodist Church Purposes